Praise for *Time to Get Real!*

"I was seeking career advice when we first met. Six months later, Alex Plinio and his Life and Career Planning Model had changed my life. Not only did he help me navigate the road to an amazing new position, the model ensured that the road led to a balanced and joyful life. No magic here. You have to stay focused, do the work, and trust the process. If you do, the result will be transformative. I know. I've never been happier, more financially secure, or more satisfied by work that is grounded in mission and aligned with personal values. Thank you, Alex."

—Dr. Ross Danis, President and CEO, MeckEd

"Alex Plinio helped me to define where I wanted to take my professional and personal career, and his Life & Career Planning Model was an effective tool that helped me reach those goals and the level of success I am at today. I myself am a coach working to educate and empower others, and similar to the thought as to who cuts a barber's hair, I'm frequently asked who coached and encouraged me. I recognize Alex for the objective voice that he was when I was caught up in what I felt I should focus on, and he provided me with great clarity to guide me on my path and challenged me when I was off-base. He allowed me to pull the treasure out from within, and for that I am forever grateful."

—Todd Polyniak, CPA, Partner, SAX Tax and Advisory Firm

"If you've ever questioned yourself or your decisions, the Life & Career Planning Model is a sneak attack on that often undermining voice in your head. This Model taught me at pivotal points, in my personal and professional life, to first identify my curiosities, what makes me tick, what I see for myself and, then, pursue them with gusto. Working with Alex brought out my inner risk-taker. I had operated from a place of fear, rather than evaluating opportunities based on my core values, interests and goals. Life & Career Planning is a road map to unearth your authentic self and happiness."

—Margaret Della, Executive Director,
Kingsbridge Heights Community Center

"A life coach and career planner for any of us is a difficult role. We change, our vision, dreams, reality changes, and yet we seek advice that crosses those borders and satisfies the moving parts. Alex Plinio is the magician with insight, sensitivity and the gut and grit to tell you the truth. He cuts across those borders, helps one identify their own blind spots, and like a great Sherpa, leads one to discover her or his own solution. His methodology is participatory, makes great sense, and provides seeable, touchable roadmaps to satisfaction and/or success. I have worked with Alex to solve corporate dilemmas while working in the pharmaceutical industry, the utility business and the arts. He has also provided me with guidance and mentoring when my ethics did not mesh with the desires of others. And then there is the personal goals piece. Alex turned me on to my own intuition, using his coaching skills. He led me to be a more confident leader and listener. He isn't just providing advice; he is providing the advice in our own words. We flatten the path; he shows us its existence."

—Ellen Lambert, retired, Chief Diversity Officer, Foundation
President, and Senior Director of Corporate Citizenship and Culture,
PSEG Services Corporation

"Life isn't always perfect but it's possible to create and live out your true mission and vision. With Alex Plinio's guidance and life and career planning seminar I was able to constructively think through big career decisions to ensure the best possible outcome. When I was considering a new career step I made sure to reflect on his planning model. I knew that a step back in my career wasn't going to be an easy decision, but it was the right one which ultimately launched me forward and into a rewarding career path. I can truly say that because of his work I consider myself grounded and happier with my life, both personally and professionally."

—Dana Bochna, Senior Partner, Early Talent Acquisition,
Human Resources, Prudential Financial

"Alex Plinio's enduringly good business judgment, organizational wherewithal and personal leadership sensitivities are among his most extraordinary attributes. He routinely combines a remarkable intersectional understanding of both the for-profit and not-for-profit worlds, including each's respective values, good and bad customs and leadership needs. He never fails to elevate the leader's view of his or her role in the world and potential for making a difference."

—Keith Stock, Chairman & CEO, First Financial Investors Inc.

Time to Get Real!

Time to Get Real!

Turning Uncertainty into an Action Plan for Personal and Professional Success

Alex J. Plinio and Melissa A. Smith

Rutgers University Press

New Brunswick, Camden, and Newark, New Jersey, and London

Library of Congress Cataloging-in-Publication Data
Names: Plinio, Alex J., author. | Smith, Melissa A., 1960– author.
Title: Time to get real! : turning uncertainty into an action plan for personal
and professional success / by Alex J. Plinio and Melissa A. Smith.
Description: New Brunswick : Rutgers University Press, [2019] |
Includes bibliographical references.
Identifiers: LCCN 2019006128 | ISBN 9781978804616 (hbk : alk. paper) |
ISBN 9781978804630 (E-pub) | ISBN 9781978804654 (web pdf) | ISBN 9781978804647 (mobi)
Subjects: LCSH: Self-control. | Self-management (Psychology) | Success. | Uncertainty.
Classification: LCC BF632 .P58 2019 | DDC 153.8—dc23
LC record available at https://lccn.loc.gov/2019006128

A British Cataloging-in-Publication record for this book is available from the British Library.

∞ The paper used in this publication meets the requirements of the American National Standard for
Information Sciences—Permanence of Paper for Printed Library Materials, ANSI Z39.48-1992.

www.rutgersuniversitypress.org

Manufactured in the United States of America

To my wife, Rose Marie, for her strong support and unending encouragement over the many years of my career; to my two sons, Steven and Mark, who taught me a great deal and who have always made me proud of the men they have become; to my mother and her optimistic view of the world with all of its human diversity; and to my father and his unwavering belief in the value of education
—Alex Plinio

To my husband, Joel, for his wisdom, insight, and support and for being my biggest cheerleader; and to my daughters, Anne and Jane, and stepchildren, Sam, Hannah, and Noah, who all have brought me great joy and pride with their accomplishments
—Melissa Smith

Contents

PART III Putting It All Together Using All Aspects of
Your Self, Work, and Career to Create a Future
That You Can Plan and Work Toward

Time to Get Real!

Introduction

Get the Best Life, the Best Career, and the Best You!

"I'm so sick of my job. I really need to do something else." "I was laid off ten months ago, and I still can't find work. What else can I do?" "I am so tired of running all the time to keep up—and I feel like I'm failing at work and at home." "I've gone from job to job, but what do I really want to do?" "I am a successful executive, and yet I feel somehow there's more for me." "How do I know what career options I have to live the life that I want?" "Retirement is not that far off, and I haven't even thought about it."

These are the voices of the people we coach and teach. They range in age from twenty-one to sixty-five. Many are at a crossroads. They are anxious to get their careers and lives in order but feel stuck. Some are executives in good jobs but feeling unfulfilled. Others are managers who feel trapped where they are. Almost all appear busy and stressed. Some hold two or more jobs; others are out of work and feeling desperate. A lack of personal fulfillment, financial worries, and fear of the unknown keep them up at night. Many feel victimized by their circumstances—betrayed by the economy, company layoffs, personal responsibilities that have to be managed, or lack of sufficient financial resources for retirement. Still others are just starting out on their career journeys. They all desperately want to have control of their lives.

Our message to them, and to you, is clear: It's *Time to Get Real!* You can be more in control than you believe and can achieve success and personal happiness, but you need to think and act like the chief executive officer (CEO) of your own life. This is the essence of *Time to Get Real!* Be that CEO.

You chose this book for a reason. There are important things on your mind that you need to think about and perhaps some other things about which you need to find resolution. Hopefully you are excited that you are about to take a step into your future. We will help guide you through the process of taking control and moving forward in a direction that brings satisfaction and life's rewards.

Our life and career planning process is different than almost anything you may have tried in the past. After many years of refining our program, we have received quite a bit of feedback about the kinds of issues against which most people struggle. Your needs are not so different from the needs of so many others we have coached, who were willing to put in the time and effort that provided the direction and plans that were needed at that time in their life. It's your turn.

We all know that effective organizations continually review, evaluate, and refine their action plans for success through a process called "strategic thinking and planning." The CEO and others in the organization periodically take a candid look at the company's strengths and weaknesses, opportunities and challenges, finances and competitive set in a changing marketplace to plan for action to better control their future. Good companies are also opportunistic. They look for those actions that can be taken now to improve their positions. How ironic that this activity happens all the time in our workplaces, yet few people consider the same approach or model for their own lives! *Time to Get Real!* takes this observation to its logical next step: the need to create a strategic plan for one's life while being assertive about the opportunities that arise each day.

Alex was thirty-four years old before he took control. We'll tell you about that later in the book. For now, know that whether you are twenty-four, forty-four, or sixty-four, it's never too early or too late to create a focus that examines your life and career and drives both of them forward in a positive way. Frankly, we both wish that each of us had started thinking about these things when we were just out of college. But it sometimes takes a while to realize that you are stuck or lack direction and control. For example, one client, Joel, sought us out when he was sixty-four years old. He needed a bridge for his last few years of work and a safe arrival to a productive retirement. In contrast, at the relatively young age of thirty-four, Alex realized he needed to accelerate his career and plan for a better life. Needs vary, but the process for meeting needs does not.

This book will direct you through the process of being the CEO of your life, turning malaise, fear, or uncertainty into an action plan for personal and professional success. Although no one can predict the future, anyone can pursue a course of his or her own design to find more happiness. Reading this book is not a quick fix, but it can be *the* fix. There are no overnight tricks to finding true insight. The real trick is to invest thought, time, and effort in developing a meaningful and disciplined plan that will enable you to weather unforeseen challenges with resilience, confidence, and self-direction while at the same time helping you to make choices as opportunities present themselves. Deep self-assessment and reflection can be uncomfortable and are not easy. They may trigger thoughts that you have avoided dealing with, resulting in inaction and "feeling stuck." The ultimate purpose of *Time to Get Real!* is to help individuals better understand their life and career and how they are integrated and to move from being stuck to developing an action plan to being where they want to be for their life and career. We have found that intelligent and thoughtful individuals can make an early mistake in thinking about what to do next. They simply want to get going, to take action, to start their search, to move ahead no matter what. This is a huge mistake, resulting from a lack of readiness and preparation. Instead, working diligently through our Life & Career Planning Model prepares you for the action that will deliver results.

Time to Get Real! originated from the lessons that Alex gained from his many years of experience as a CEO, business and thought leader, educator, and life/career coach to help people from all walks of life realize their full potential. Life and career planning became a personal mission for Alex more than thirty years ago, while on a retreat for a board of directors on which he served. The board chair was John W. Gardner, president of the Carnegie Corporation when he was tapped by President Lyndon Johnson to serve as secretary of

Health, Education, and Welfare implementing the reforms of Johnson's Great Society. Later, Gardner went on to found both Common Cause, a nonpartisan grass-roots organization dedicated to upholding the core values of American democracy, and Independent Sector, a coalition of nonprofits, foundations, and corporate giving programs, while serving on various nonprofit and corporate boards, including those of Shell Oil Company, American Airlines, the Metropolitan Museum of Art, and Stanford University. He was an excellent human being with strong personal values, a true Renaissance man, and a role model. There were about fifteen board members at the retreat, and John wanted them to focus on self-renewal, a subject he had written extensively about in various books on leadership.

John asked each of them, all executives heading up various organizations, if those organizations had a specific mission, vision, strategic plan, and goals. All of the members responded, "Yes, of course." He then asked if they, as individuals, had a documented, written mission, vision, strategic plan, and goals for their own lives. Almost to a person, fourteen out of fifteen of the board members cast a downward glance and responded, "No." This was a stunning realization to Alex—how absurd and risky it was that he was "winging" this most important aspect of his life. He realized he was caring and planning more for his organization than for his own life. From there, he began to craft a planning model and put it to work for himself. This was enormously empowering, and Alex began to evangelize the idea to others. This grew into a lifelong passion for mentoring and coaching, and this book is the ultimate result of Alex's drive to share and extend the lessons he learned along the way.

As CEO of Prudential Annuity Services, a billion-dollar revenue business, and president of both the Prudential Foundation and the American Field Service, an international nonprofit that helps to exchange students in the United States and fifty other countries, Alex realized that this methodology worked cross-culturally as well, and he started training executives, managers, and students in his approach. These insights about the power of personal planning and the responsibilities of leadership led him to cofound the Institute for Ethical

Leadership and the Center for Nonprofit and Philanthropic Leadership at Rutgers Business School. Here, trainers focus on a broad cross-section of leaders from business, government, and nonprofit organizations, as well as undergraduate and graduate students. In addition, Alex opened a consulting practice and later teamed with Melissa Smith to found the company Life & Career Planning, LLC. Alex began to think about writing this book in conjunction with the work of the company and linking it to the various methods of self-help and direct help that he and Melissa might provide, both in person and through the use of today's technological advances. This concept aligns directly with Alex's life purpose, which is to "help individuals and organizations to become what they seek to become while encouraging them to discern and understand their full potential and to have the courage to strive towards that potential."

Melissa's story is quite different from Alex's. She managed her career within one organization for a number of years learning sales, marketing, training, operations, and sales management. Gaining skills in these various areas helped her rise through the ranks and become the vice president of sales. She realized that the people reporting to her needed ongoing guidance and coaching because it was not possible for her to be successful and achieve sales targets or other goals unless she did it through well-trained and motivated people. This interest in and ability to develop people to be their best helped her achieve her business goals, and she eventually earned the role of division president. As her children entered their teen years and her vision for her own life evolved, Melissa began looking for a shift in purpose and priorities. She just happened to see Alex being interviewed on a television show, where he discussed how to use the Life & Career Planning Model. Melissa soon decided on a career change, left her position as president of Aerosoles Shoes retail stores, and became the executive director of the Institute for Ethical Leadership at Rutgers Business School, working directly with Alex. In this role, she was able to train and coach many business and nonprofit leaders and students, as well as to teach life and career planning using the model. As part of her own life and career plan, she also earned an MBA from Rutgers Business School.

A few years ago, Melissa again decided to shift her goals, vision, and life plan and used the Life & Career Planning Model to do so. She is now a leadership and business consultant growing Life & Career Planning, LLC with Alex.

Alex and Melissa designed *Time to Get Real!* to be used as an accessible reference and resource—large enough to write in, small enough to comfortably carry in a briefcase, handbag, or book bag. Chapters in the book contain powerful coaching tips and prompts, writing and thought exercises, real-life scenarios, personal anecdotes, relevant charts and data, and encouraging quotes and references that drive the reader forward. *Time to Get Real!* moves from chapter to chapter easily, with no rehash or repetition, but instead each section introduces new ideas for you the reader to consider on your path toward your new life.

We are compelled to write this book now because the stakes are simply too high to ignore. Surviving and thriving in this new economy demands a disciplined, enduring approach to one's personal life and career management. The recession that started in 2007 wreaked havoc on millions of people in the United States and around the world. Now, at this writing, we appear to be in an economic recovery. However, political and economic winds continue to create uncertainty about the future of the country and the world. Sailing your ship in this environment requires more knowledge, thought, and planning, so that one is always tacking in the right direction. The pace of change in our country and the world, whether political, social, or economic, can at times be turbulent, requiring one's hand to always be on the rudder.

According to 2018 statistics released by the US Department of Labor, of the 145.5 million Americans in the workforce, approximately 6.6 million—about 4 percent—are still jobless, mainly because of ongoing economic changes beyond their control. An additional 4.7 million of us are "underemployed," many working part-time because they are unable to find full-time work.[1]

Alex vividly recalls listening to his university president speak at his graduation ceremony. The president said, "Many of you students have a father who probably spent more than twenty-five or thirty years in the same job." That certainly was the case for Alex. The president went on to say that the students sitting in front of him would most likely have at least four separate employers or distinctly different positions. That became true for both Alex and Melissa. The velocity of this job churn has only increased with time. In this new reality, the average person born in the later years of the Baby Boom (1946–1964) holds 11.7 jobs between the ages of eighteen and forty-two, according to the findings in a longitudinal study released in August 2017 by the Bureau of Labor Statistics of the Department of Labor.[2] Living with this level of change, uncertainty, and insecurity can be crippling.

Succeeding in this new economy takes a lot more than luck and playing by the rules. It requires that you approach your life like an astute leader to create your own strategic action plan, a safe harbor to weather the velocity of change and propel you toward a personally successful future. It means you have to get real—and now is the time. Because if you do nothing, the unknown future will control you, like it or not.

Gregory worked for a global company for a number of years and thought he was on a firm career track. However, the company was acquired, and he was abruptly given a severance package. This unexpected shift created a tremendous upheaval in his life, and it took Gregory six months to figure out where he was headed next. By focusing on his personal vision and values and developing clear goals and plans, he created a consulting firm, developed his own product, and is now working to grow his thriving business. Gregory is but one person like so many others who have faced swift currents and were able to tack their boat in a positive direction.

There are others, of course, not ready and not prepared, who when faced with unexpected changes drift or drown. A friend of Alex's owned his own business. He was doing quite well. However, when the economy tanked, his product was not in the "necessity" category. Unfortunately, luxury goods and services are the first things to be cut from a shrinking household budget. He thought that his business would grow and go on forever. He was wrong. The business collapsed, and he was without a job for two years. He finally got back on his feet by working for someone else. He had no contingency plan because he was comfortable believing that things would continue to be great forever. The lesson here is that having a life and career plan is a requirement in both good and bad times.

It's time for you to get new information about your situation. Some of this knowledge will come from external sources, while some comes from within you. No one should be foolish enough to think he or she can plan for the future without a base of facts on which to draw. Some answers to key questions will be easy to obtain: Do I have a financial plan? What are my strengths and areas I need to develop? Others will not be so easy: Can I own up to resolving a toxic relationship in my life? Do I need to make a career change to get what I want? This process may make you uncomfortable at times. But that's okay. Remember that feeling tension is not a bad thing. One way or the other, resolution is a product of resolved tension.

Not surprisingly, executive and career coaching services are in higher demand than ever. Executive coaching is currently a billion-dollar industry.[3] According to the Stanford Graduate School of Business 2013 Executive Coaching Survey, nearly 66 percent of CEOs currently do not receive coaching or leadership advice from outside consultants or coaches, while 100 percent of them stated that they are receptive to making changes based on feedback. Nearly 80 percent of directors said that their CEO is receptive to coaching.[4] We can say without equivocation that our experience has shown an acute need at all ages and income levels for life advice and career coaching.

When Alex was appointed president of American Field Service–USA, he hired an executive coach. Sounds weird right? The man who developed the Life & Career Planning Model felt that he could benefit from coaching! Well, it isn't weird, because a coach's perspective, unbiased and unvarnished, can help you to make decisions about the work you're engaged in, the people you work with, or whether it might be time to move on to something else.

When Melissa was president of Aerosoles retail, the company was on a fast growth track. In order to handle an unusual growth spurt and to help her balance her job and her life, she worked with her human resources department to hire a coach with relevant experience in working with executives in high-growth environments. Both Melissa and the company thrived in the new environment.

For those millions of people unable to access or afford professional counseling, as well as for those eager and willing to use personal resources to obtain it, *Time to Get Real!* fills a void and provides a crucial service. Its basic and fundamental approach can be deployed at any adult life stage. But for those who are stuck, in transition, or at a pivotal life moment like graduation, choosing a career, changing jobs, losing a job, marrying, starting a family, contemplating divorce, deciding on a midlife career change, approaching retirement, *it's vital.* There are eighty million Millennials who live and work amid constant innovation and change and sixty-three million Gen Xers who seek more work-life balance than that of their parents. There is also the army of seventy-five million Baby Boomers whose lives of economic prosperity have left them ill prepared for ether a bust economy or the number of job changes the economy calls for, as well as the twenty-seven million Americans born before 1945 who are living longer, many on finite resources. The members of each of these population sectors must confront their own reality to turn their dreams into an enduring action plan that can achieve their desired results. *Time to Get Real!* is the spark that can light your fire. In other words, through use of the Life & Career Planning Model, as outlined in this book, various aspects of one's work and career are highlighted, reviewed, and improved.

Time to Get Real! is the work of two individuals who have traveled the road between the business, nonprofit, and government sectors while serving in leadership positions. We write about what we know, and what we know is extremely important information for individuals seeking to enhance their careers and their lives in holistic ways. In addition, both of us have taught at the undergraduate and graduate levels, served on boards of directors, and been lifetime volunteers for the causes in which we believe.

Our aim is to help individuals as much as we possibly can. Therefore, this book does not stand alone. You can also take advantage of our telephonic coaching, blogs, webinars, retreats, and seminars, if needed. We worked with Thomas Edison State University, a major provider of online courses for adult learners, to develop and launch a course solely focused on our copywrited Life and Career Planning Model. You will find in the book's resource section our contact information as well as information on other resources you can turn to for more support. This book can be used alone, but you are not alone if you choose not to be; this is entirely up to you.

Alex and Melissa both utilize their life and career planning knowledge and experience through their consulting firm but also in their personal lives. When you complete your life and career planning process, you too may find that you can help others as a result of your experience. For example, Alex helped a family member to negotiate and make a career change within a large, global company. This person wanted to move from one department to another and, with Alex's advice, negotiated a six-month trial period in that new department, which eventually led him to change his role within the company. Alex also helped another family member to understand that during the depths of the 2008 recession, making precipitous decisions about financial matters would not bode well for his future since he was young and needed to better understand how financial markets work. By discussing this individual's financial plans and goals, it became evident that panicking at that time would be the worst thing to do.

There may be times when you too can become a coach in a specific situation by using parts of the Life & Career Planning Model to help other individuals in your life. Imagine the advantage you will have when completing all parts of the model and knowing where you are and where you are going. This will place you ahead of many individuals in your peer group.

Julia, a client, approached us when she felt stuck in her job and wanted to figure out what her next move would be. She used the plan that she developed to formulate the answers that she would give to questions asked of her during new job interviews. Because of the work she had done through the Life & Career Planning Model, she was able to immediately understand how her values and vision might fit into a new company. She was also prepared to answer questions about how much compensation she could afford to accept. She was also able to ask questions about the company's employee development programs to determine if those programs might meet her own learning needs because she had thought through what her own learning needs were. Finally, life balance was important to Julia, and she was able to be very direct with her questions to interviewers to find out if the company's culture and climate would provide the environment she sought for her own life balance.

In sum, while there is enormous need for coaching and counsel on life and career planning, achieving balance, and working toward personal success, few books bring to you the experiential, comprehensive, and commonsense approach that you'll find on these pages. *Time to Get Real!* provides essential life-planning tools, including the very real need for financial planning to make dreams possible. This book is a platform for anyone at any life stage but is particularly suited to those in the vortex of career loss, change, or the need to better align their life goals with career goals. By the end of the book, you will have an action plan to hold fast to, one that responds to change—for a lifetime.

What differentiates our book, our life and career planning process, and all our corollary aids from what has been available in the marketplace to this point is a two-stage focus that you will follow. First, the Life & Career Planning Model is elegantly simple, easy to follow, and interesting in which to engage. It is a useful tool. However, second, *you* are in control and fully responsible for model inputs and outputs, while being guided by proven expertise. You can go through the material and the steps quickly or slowly, but you must engage in the entire process and spend time, effort, and thought to get the payoff you desire.

To make this process meaningful and productive for you, we want to outline the ground rules that will help each reader have a meaningful experience with this book and our model and be able to carry that experience into the future.

Ground Rules

- This is not a book just to be read. This is a book requiring focus, attention, and work on your part.

- The book contains examples of how we suggest you document the journey on which you are embarking. Documentation not only becomes important for the initial learning experience but also creates a framework around which future revision of your plan can take place. A completed plan provides a decision-making template against which life's options can be chosen after ascertaining the alignment of one's decision with a desired future. You will be able to refer to your plan documentation at various points in your life when there is a need to go back to your thinking and to focus on what is important to you.

- If you get stuck for any reason, there are other resources you can consult and use alongside this book. First, you need the courage to consult with your key relationships to obtain unvarnished input and advice on your plan. Second, you can always get further advice from Alex and Melissa through their telephone coaching, blogs, emails, retreats, and other resources that they make available through the website Lifeandcareerplanning.com. In addition, you can utilize many of the other resources noted in the book's "Resources" section. Using this book to develop your plan should be sufficient. However, never hesitate, when needed, to seek help from the people close to you or from the authors.

- The reading and the doing will take time. You must recognize that to arrive at your life and career plan, the timing is all in your hands. If you want to better control your life, you need to better control your planning, but the speed at which you work through the steps in this book is all up to you. Therefore, you should expect a range of potential completion times, dependent on what you put into your work and how serious or urgent your personal situation may be.

- Our experience tells us that if someone puts aside this book and one's work on the model for four or more weeks, the chances for that person completing the plan are greatly diminished. In other words, to stay on track, you should commit to working on the plan *at a minimum* every two weeks, if not more and earlier.

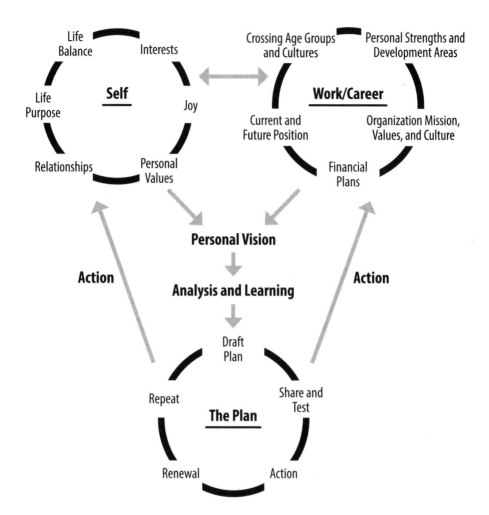

The Life & Career Planning Model

The graphic on the following page depicts the coaching model used in our teaching, presentations, and coaching. It helps people better understand the process and the road they must travel over the course of completing the work required by the model.

The coaching process starts with an examination of self, then moves to a review of work and career. Once those two parts of the model are completed, a personal vision is developed, extending out at least three to five years. After you analyze your results and what you've learned, you then develop a plan that you activate immediately and revise periodically, as circumstances of your life change.

The chapters in *Time to Get Real!* focus on each part of the model, and you will be given a short explanation at the beginning of each chapter as to that part's purpose in the model and the results you can expect once you're done working through that section.

You may find some parts of the model easy to respond to, while others can be quite difficult. By applying time and thinking through your responses, each part of the model will help you develop the primary inputs for your plan. We realize that deep thinking around such things as life's purpose, one's vision for one's life, or the next position one should take in life may be uncomfortable. But that's when you know that something important is about to occur. Let discomfort be a spark for your creativity and not an impediment. Move ahead one step at a time, and don't stop.

Bon voyage on one of the most important journeys you will experience in your lifetime.

Conscious change is brought about by the two qualities inherent in consciousness: attention and intention. Attention energizes, and intention transforms. Whatever you put your attention on will grow stronger in your life.

—Deepak Chopra, *The Seven Spiritual Laws of Success*

PART I

Self

A Review of Those Aspects of Your Life That Make You Who You Are

CHAPTER 1

Interests

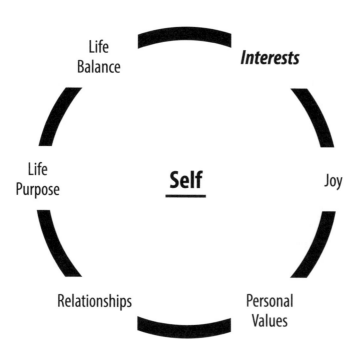

The purpose of the work to be completed in this chapter is to arrive at a point where you, the reader, better understand those things in your life that are attractive to you, are motivational, are inspirational, and make you feel good.

Let's start our journey with something easy and perhaps fun for many readers. Let's talk about what your interests are and why they are your interests.

First, let's define here what we mean by your interests. Interests are those aspects of an individual's life to which he or she is attracted. Interests may provide an outlet for creativity or a way to reduce stress, be a contributor to one's inspiration, or perhaps act as a path to feeling relaxed or happier. A *casual* interest is an intrinsically rewarding, short-lived, pleasurable activity requiring little or no preparation, such as having an interest in going to the movies for fun. If you feel like going to the movies, you can check the local theater for times, pick a film that sounds interesting in the moment, and go. A *serious* interest is the systematic pursuit of a hobby, a sport, or a volunteer activity that is a substantial time investment, provides greater rewards and satisfaction, and results in a sense of accomplishment or good feeling. To take the film example further, someone with a serious interest in film might go to the movies regularly, read film magazines, attend film festivals to search out obscure auteurs, and write reviews for a movie blog or local newspaper.

Pleasurable activity can take place in different settings. For example, you can have interest in activities you do when you're not working (e.g., travel to new places), when you're working (e.g., leading a team), when you're learning (e.g., obtaining a postgraduate degree), or, perhaps, when serving your country (e.g., military reserve or guard duty). Only you can determine what your casual and serious interests are and what their impact is on your life and well-being.

Here are some common interests that people have to help you think about what your interests might be:

- Reading books
- Meditation
- Spending quality time with family
- Spending time with pets or other animals
- Visiting parks and nature
- Music—listening to or creating
- Collecting—stamps, music, coins, etc.

- Playing or watching sports
- Watching movies
- Touring museums
- Creating art
- Eating out
- Cooking
- Exploring other cultures
- Traveling
- Photography
- Physical activity/exercise
- Contributing to charities
- Having lunch at work with associates
- Joining work or social clubs
- Taking classes or seeking a degree
- Relaxing at the beach
- Gardening
- Mentoring

Take some time for the following exercise: Make a list of at least five things in your life that are of keen interest to you. Think broadly. Whatever they are, list them.

My Interests

1. _____

2. _____

3. _____

4. _____

5. _____

Here are a few examples of responses from individuals we have coached:

When Linda was asked about her interests, she said her primary interest was travel. We asked, "Why?" She responded that she liked to visit new places. Again, "Why?" She said it helped her to learn about other people and cultures. We continued to probe: "Why is that important?" She said that it allowed her to remove herself from her own people and culture, relaxed her, was educational, and made her feel freer from whatever she left back home. So, for Linda, traveling was an exercise in freedom, relaxation, and education—a balm or salve for her very busy life.

John said that his primary interests included playing golf and going out for drinks and dinner with friends. Why? He said that golf, although individually challenging, represented a way for him to be with and bond with other men in a shared experience. We asked why that was important to him. He responded that he was single, lived alone, and enjoyed the company of other people, whether at play or at work. Why? He noted that it provided a sense of being on a team or in a family. Why? What meaning did that have for him? He said that doing things with others and not being alone all the time was important to him. So John wanted companionship, friendship, and a sense of belonging, not just a golf game and a few drinks.

After you have filled in your own five interests, let's try to discern just *why* these five things are of interest to you. To do that, ask yourself that same simple question for each one of your stated interests. Why is this particular thing of interest to me? After you have answered that question, keep asking "Why?" again three or four times, to get deeper and deeper into your motivations for being attracted to that particular thing. This questioning method will help you to get at the real reason this activity is of interest to you. It is important that you think through all of these interests, since the work you do now will tie in later to other parts of the Life & Career Planning Model and will help you to better understand your needs and desires, in both your private life and your career. As with all parts of the model, you need to write down your responses for future reference and for when we blend all the parts of the model into your vision and action plan for the future later in the process. It is very important to document your responses to each part of the model. You will need to refer back to this documentation when developing your action plan now, as well as when you need to update your plan when something in your life situation changes.

Now that you know the process, transfer the five interests you wrote down above to the box below and interrogate each one a few times until you uncover the importance of your interests to your life.

Interrogating My Interests

Interest 1. _____

Why? _____

Why? _____

Why? _____

Why? _____

Interest 2. _____

Why? _____

Why? _____

Why? _____

Why? _____

Interest 3. _____

Why? _____

Why? _____

Why? _____

Why? _____

Interest 4. _____

   Why? _____

   Why? _____

   Why? _____

   Why? _____

Interest 5. _____

   Why? _____

   Why? _____

   Why? _____

   Why? _____

When you review your responses, noting why you have these interests, do you see any themes emerging? If so, what are they? Write them down in the box on the following page. In the preceding examples, the themes that emerged for Linda were the excitement provided by learning in different cultures, becoming unattached from her familiar setting and life's stresses, and having a feeling of personal freedom. For

John, although his focus is a sport, golf, the key themes in his interest are his need for having close ties to others in a friendly environment and to overcome the feeling of loneliness in his life by connecting with other people. So what are the themes emerging in your interests?

The surest path to true happiness lies in chasing not just happiness but also a meaningful life.

**—Emily Esfahani Smith and Jennifer Aaker,
"In 2017, Pursue Meaning Instead of Happiness"**

Themes I See Emerging

1. _____

2. _____

3. _____

4. _____

5. _____

Are some of the themes found across most of your interest areas? For example, do your interest areas excite you, calm you down, make you feel stronger, get you intellectually more curious, arouse your senses, solidify relationships, or just feed your curiosity? These factors are at the core of what motivates you toward these various activities. Later we can explore them from the point of view of the work you like to do, the people you like to associate with, and the life you would like to lead.

At this point, when looking at what you have written, make sure that you have not overlooked any interests of importance to you. If you have, go back and add them to your list. Then we can move on.

Next, think about the amount of time you spend engaged in the interests that you enjoy and document that below. It is okay to use estimates. We all have different amounts of time to spend at work and at home. Some of that time is spent with family and friends, some on chores, and some on one or more of our interests.

How Much Time Do I Spend?

My Interests	Time Spent
1. _____	_____
2. _____	_____
3. _____	_____
4. _____	_____
5. _____	_____

Then, consider what activities you spend time on that are not key interests. These would be activities that are necessary for the functioning of your life but perhaps bring you little pleasure. List at least five of those, for example, talking with friends on the phone, watching television, going to the gym, volunteering, spending time on social media, shopping, reading, sleeping late, managing personal assets, cooking, and doing housework. Alex goes to the gym three or four times a week because he wants to stay healthy. However, there are some mornings that he has to drag himself out of bed to get there—not very pleasurable. But he needs it in his life, so he goes. Melissa, on the other hand, is a gym rat and belongs to a boot camp, which she happily and regularly attends. She likes it so much that she has received several awards for fitness and boxing. See the difference? For Melissa, going to the gym is a major interest; for Alex, it's something he feels he has to do but is not among his major interests.

Some people, especially in this age of social media, spend a significant amount of time on their electronic devices. Recent research indicates that there are those who almost have an addiction to the use of these technologies.[1] Their use can certainly be distracting. If you're in a relationship and your significant other has to say to you, "Please put down the phone; you are here, but you are not here," you may have to consider how your use of technology is impacting your personal life. This particular interest could create some dysfunction in your life and may need to be better controlled.

Activities I Spend Time On That Are Not Key Interests

1. _____ Why? _____

2. _____ Why? _____

3. _____ Why? _____

4. _____ Why? _____

5. _____ Why? _____

Why do you spend time on these activities? Is it habit? Doing it for someone else? People expect it of you? Are there clear reasons for you to engage in this activity? If not, would it be easy or difficult to disengage? Document your responses for each activity.

For example, James volunteers for a nonprofit organization. When asked why, he said he wanted to give back to his community. When asked if he enjoyed volunteering for this organization, he said, "Not really." When asked why he felt that way, he said that the time he was spending helping this social service organization was not exceptionally fulfilling. When asked why it wasn't fulfilling, he said the volunteering was in an area in which he had little interest, but the volunteer work was easy. When asked what he might be interested in instead, he said he was very interested in the creative arts. From there we began to talk about what it might take for him to stop volunteering in the social services organization and to find a way to volunteer for a creative arts organization. In other words, some people migrate down the road that's easiest to walk down rather than focusing on the path that will help them to arrive at a place more suited to their real interests and therefore more appealing. By interrogating why you are participating in activities that do not revolve around your core interests, you may uncover some surprising insights, as James did.

Some interests are really habits hiding as interests. For example, has your smartphone become a part of your hand? Are your eyes glued to the television? Do you really have to get up that late or go to bed that early? Do you always eat at the same place and have the same thing for lunch? Why?

Here are some averages for how Americans spend their time on daily leisure.

Leisure Time on an Average Day

Activity	Minutes Spent
Watching TV	167 (2.8 hours)
Socializing and communicating	41
Playing games; using computer for leisure	25
Reading	19
Sports, exercise, and recreation	18
Relaxing and thinking	17
Other leisure activities	12
Total leisure and sports time (5.0 hours)	299

Note: Data include all persons age fifteen and over. Data include all days of the week and are annual averages for 2015.

Source: Bureau of Labor Statistics, "2016 American Time Use Survey," June 27, 2017, https://www.bls.gov/news.release/archives/atus_06272017.htm.

Finally, consider the reasons or feelings that prevent you from moving away from nonpleasurable interests toward those that are more meaningful and enjoyable for you. Common responses to this questioning include "I don't have the time," I don't have the money," "I work long hours," and "My family comes first." However, if you desire change in your life, then your action has to be intentional. And the first step in changing your behavior is uncovering the motivations behind why you are still participating in the activities that make up your life.

At this point, you have documented your areas of interest as well as those activities that you engage in that are not very interesting or are a form of habit. Take a look at each activity on these lists, and prioritize the interests that you would like to engage in even more and prioritize those "interests or habits" that you need to work on or reduce.

What are they?

Interests That I Plan to Prioritize as More Important

1. _____

2. _____

3. _____

4. _____

5. _____

Interests or Habits That I Plan to Reduce or Eliminate

1. _____

2. _____

3. _____

4. _____

5. _____

Later, when we begin the analysis and learning part of the model and direct our attention to developing the plan, these insights will become action areas and coordinated or tied into other aspects of the model.

For now, you should have learned the following:

- You should know what interests you have and why you have them.
- You should recognize you are spending time in some areas that are not productive and not really of interest to you.
- You should also have developed a commitment toward making changes that are more productive for your life.

As you explored your interests, you may have had some insights or maybe even an "aha" experience. The box below will help you to capture those insights for later reference.

What Have I Learned by Exploring My Interests?

_____

_____

_____

_____

_____

_____

_____

_____

Although we're not entering the planning phases yet, it would be helpful for you to jot down right now three or four things that you believe might be part of your action plan, steps that you would take, as a result of what you have learned about your interests.

Ideas for My Action Plan

1. _____

2. _____

3. _____

4. _____

Do these potential actions seem realistic? Are they enough to move you toward the things that are of interest in your life? Are you too easy on yourself?

Your focus and attention have produced some solid information for you to be able to bridge to the next part of the Life & Career Planning Model. The next chapter, which focuses on what gives you joy in your life, when combined with the work that you have done on your interests, will begin to form the early part of the picture of what happiness looks like to you. After all, in a sea of change, being comfortable in our own skin and in a place in our life that gives us equilibrium is a worthy goal.

CHAPTER 2

Joy

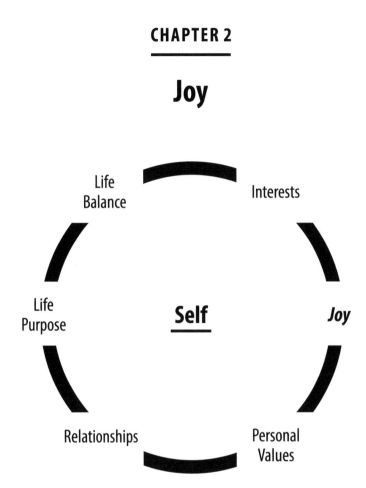

The purpose of the work to be completed in this chapter is to arrive at a point where you, the reader, understand those things in your life that have brought you feelings of joy and what you might do to re-create those feelings.

In chapter 1, we focused on the interests in your life and why they are so interesting to you. Now we're going to dive a bit deeper. Together we are going to explore what has brought joy to your life. What do we mean by joy? Joy is experienced in multiple ways: a sense of accomplishment, a feeling of happiness, being outside yourself with a sense of exhilaration, or the prospect of possessing what one desires. This sense of joy is very personal. Joy is derived in different ways for different people. However, we all know that when we have it, we like it a lot and would love to keep it. Joy can come from various sources: your work, your interests, your family, your hobbies, things accomplished, challenges overcome, new experiences, and so on.

Your success and happiness lies in you. Resolve to keep happy, and your joy and you shall form an invincible host against difficulties.

—Helen Keller

To the extent possible, the more we can replicate in our life and in our careers that feeling of joy, the happier we will be. Can we do it consciously? The answer is yes. According to the happiness researcher Sonja Lyubomirsky, of the University of California–Riverside, "the benefits of happiness include higher income and superior work outcomes, larger social rewards, more activity, energy, and flow, better physical health, and even longer life."[1] Dr. Lyubomirsky has found that happy individuals are more creative, helpful, charitable, and self-confident, have better self-control, and show greater self-regulatory and coping abilities.

Let's start with an important exercise. Looking back on your life, what achievement or life occurrences gave you the most joy? Document, in the area provided on pages 36–37, six to eight of these occurrences in a couple of paragraphs or a list that you can refer back to later. Some experiences provide a sense of accomplishment; others provide a high degree of learning or experiential feedback. Some joyful experiences are one-time events, for example, the birth of a child. Other joyful experiences may be ongoing, such as your annual two-week family vacation at the beach. It is important to document all of your work for each of the parts of the Life & Career Planning Model, since you will return to that documentation when formulating your action plan later and when you update it in the future. Before you start writing on pages 36–37, here are a few examples.

In using the Life & Career Planning Model for the very first time to think about joy in Alex's life, he documented twelve different achievements, occurrences, and experiences that brought him joy. The number itself isn't important. What's important is what created the joy in Alex's life and why it was created. One of the first things that Alex wrote down was how the birth of his two sons provided a tremendous amount of joy in his life, not only at the time of their birth but also as their lives have helped to weave the fabric of his own life stronger and better over time. That event, their birth, created a family for Alex and his wife, Rose Marie, which to this very day is central to Alex's life and certainly continues to provide him with an ongoing sense of joy.

A second example that Alex documented occurred when he was president of the Prudential Foundation, a nonprofit charitable entity funded by Prudential Financial to make grants and manage social investments focused on specific areas of interest. At the time, the need for housing in the city of Newark, New Jersey, was acute. Only ten units of new housing had been built in the preceding twenty years. As vice president of public affairs, Alex had substantial resources at his disposal in the Prudential Foundation and in the Prudential Social Investment Fund. He thought he might be able to use those resources as part of Prudential's corporate social responsibility to spark home building in the city. He worked with a minority developer, and Prudential invested in forty new units of housing in the central area of the city—an area that had been devastated by the 1967 civil rebellion. Many people thought the company was crazy for investing the money in such a neighborhood. However, after building and selling the forty initial units and attracting a major home-building developer,

Hovnanian, which later became a partner with the minority developer, together they put up over three hundred units of new housing, which are well maintained and still exist today. The feeling of joy that Alex experienced by doing this work was multifaceted. First, homes were being provided to middle-class families in the heart of the city. Second, Prudential actually made money on their sale. Third, the naysayers were proven wrong. Fourth, a small investment in the area attracted the larger Hovnanian investment, and finally, on behalf of his employer, Alex was able to make a social contribution to Newark, a city where he was born and raised and where Prudential was founded and headquartered. He felt happy and satisfied every time he looked out his office window and saw those homes.

Peter, one of our coaching clients, asked us why he had to focus so much on his personal joy. He came to us to move his career ahead and didn't see the connection between his personal feelings and his job. The answer to that question for everyone, not only Peter, is that what you're searching for in your life and in your work is the very same feeling you get from your interests and from your experiences of joy. If we know what triggers these emotions in your life, we just might be able to find a way to replicate those feelings in what you do in your life and career—or, at least, to get closer.

Find out where joy resides, and give it a voice far beyond singing. For to miss the joy is to miss all.

—Robert Louis Stevenson

Just one quick example of a person who was able to merge her life and work to focus on her interests and achieve joy: Vivian was about to leave a job, not of her own volition. When going through the Life & Career Planning Model with her, we discerned that she had a high degree of interest in scuba diving, and she experienced a great deal of joy when she went on a scuba-diving adventure, especially when that trip included people with disabilities. She was an excellent guide and trainer. She had spent most of her adult career managing programs and small business. Guess what? Today she teaches scuba diving at a university, and she has a business that plans and develops scuba-diving trips with small groups. She is much happier now that her career aligns with her interests, and she gets to work in an area that brings her much joy. That's why this approach of thinking about things we often take for granted in our lives can help us later when we get to parts of the model that look at your current and future career position or ask you to develop a personal vision for the future driven by your values.

In Melissa's case, gardening brings her joy. Every spring she begins planning in advance, studying gardening journals and catalogues, listing the plants she wants to add that year for specific goals, such as attracting butterflies or humming birds. Going to the plant nursery is a joyful experience for Melissa, as she goes up and down each row of plants, carefully choosing specimens and marking items off her list. The next few days spent in planting are especially exhilarating as she digs in the dirt and watches the garden take shape. As the season progresses, Melissa derives more joy from walking around her yard with family and friends, naming species and observing the flowers blooming and thriving. For her, this is an ongoing, annual experience. The reason Melissa finds joy in gardening is because it is a creative experience that allows her to connect with nature, it is a form of exercise, and gardening has a tangible result that can be enjoyed by many people.

To spark your thinking, here is a starter list of some things that can create joy:

- Completing a difficult work assignment
- Playing or watching sports
- Working on a do-it-yourself project at home
- Being philanthropic
- Receiving a compensation increase because of your quality performance
- Learning a new skill, e.g., cooking, a language, painting, etc.
- Making something with your own hands
- Planning and taking a family vacation

- Helping others
- Entertaining people at a social event
- Meditating
- Mentoring a colleague at work
- Being awarded stock options beyond your expectation
- Changing career fields and doing well in the new career
- Spending time outdoors
- Leading a team and accomplishing a goal

Now it's your turn. Please write one or two paragraphs on your own, describing the achievements and occurrences that gave you the most joy. Describe the event and how it made you feel. Then go further and describe *why* you felt the way that you did.

For now, you may want to use this scaffolding, but feel free to write it out on your own paper or personal computer as well.

My Experiences of Joy

In my life, one of my joyous experiences occurred when the following happened:

_____

_____

_____

I felt joy when having the following achievement:

_____

_____

_____

Other experiences or occurrences of joy:

_____

_____

_____

_____

_____

_____

_____

_____

We know that it is not easy for some people to do such intense reflection into their own lives, but the model works best when you have more than one or two of your joyous experiences documented. Strive to recognize times when you felt happy—when things were going well, when you accomplished something meaningful to you, when everything just clicked. Not everything will be a burst of emotion. Sometimes joy is quieter, as in Alex's Prudential example. Think through all the various aspects of your life for these moments.

Sometimes themes emerge once you have everything written down. Do you see any in your own list? In Alex's case, many of the things that he wrote about had to do with making a contribution to people's lives, businesses, or communities. Other people might say that the personal recognition that they received from their experiences was quite motivating. Still others might say that what brought them joy was a life-changing experience. It's important to note that it doesn't matter whether others know about these experiences or know that they gave you joy; it's solely important that *you* recognize it. Do you see any distinctive characteristics or central subjects in the experiences or instances that provided you with joy? List them here.

Themes

_____

_____

_____

_____

_____

_____

_____

_____

As you look at what you've described in this chapter and compare it to the interests you listed in chapter 1, you may find similarities or overlaps that help you understand what generates these important, joyful feelings of self-satisfaction, peace, and exhilaration. When we complete the Analysis and Learning part of the plan later, we will tie in the findings from these first two sections of the plan to the actions that you'll be taking to create the life and career environments that will keep you motivated, interested, and happy.

We're sure that thinking about what brings you joy created some learning for you. What were those lessons? List them in the box below.

What Have I Learned by Exploring What Brings Me Joy?

_____

_____

_____

_____

_____

_____

_____

_____

_____

_____

Please document any ideas that you might have gleaned from doing this exercise that could be considered later when we start to develop your plan.

Ideas for My Action Plan

1. _____

2. _____

3. _____

4. _____

Molly Sims, in an article she wrote for *O—Oprah Magazine* titled "What Would Make You Happy?," noted that a Yale psychology professor, Laurie Santos, using measurable research, had created a course that nearly 25 percent of Yale undergraduates attended. It was the most popular in the school's history. Santos believes we are entitled to and capable of much more joy than we've settled for. The data suggest that becoming happier is a lot like learning to play the violin. You just have to commit to practicing.

About 50 percent of our happiness is genetic, Santos told Simms. "So yes, some people are predisposed to being unhappy, and they may not think it's worth it to seek out things that could make them feel better." But "only 10 percent of [our mood] is dictated . . . by what happens to us, . . . [while] 40 percent of our happiness is under our conscious control. . . . It's just a matter of doing the work."[2]

When I began writing the "The Happiness Hypothesis," I believed that
happiness came from within, . . . but by the time I finished writing,
I had changed my mind. Happiness comes from between. It comes from
getting the right relationships between yourself and others, yourself
and your work, yourself and something larger than yourself.

—Jonathan Haidt, *The Righteous Mind*

Whether you know it or not, what drives you in your life and in the work that you do and how you do it are your personal values. As we approach the next part of the Life & Career Planning Model, which focuses on values, you will begin to see the connection that values have with your experiences of joy and your interests. These three aspects of your life form the engine that will propel you forward toward your desired future.

CHAPTER 3

Personal Values

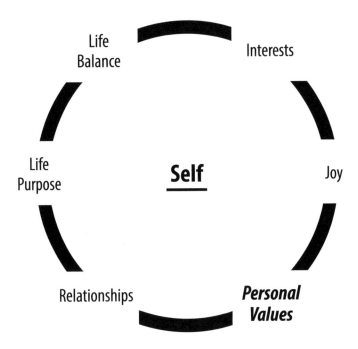

Life
Balance

Interests

Life
Purpose

Self

Joy

Relationships

*Personal
Values*

The purpose of this chapter is to have you recognize and understand your personal values, their importance, and how they impact your career and your life.

Ethan was a friend of Alex's and a longtime educator in public high schools. He eventually became the principal of a large high school. Ethan always talked about the need for young people to have strong personal values to move their lives forward in a positive direction. Honesty, respect for others, and focus on family were among the many things he would mention in the conversations he and Alex had.

One day they were purchasing something in a store, and as they paid for their purchases and moved beyond the register, Ethan looked at Alex and said, "Look at this: the cashier mistakenly gave me a twenty-dollar bill for change instead of a one-dollar bill." Alex responded, "Guess you'd better let her know." Ethan said, "Are you kidding?" and exited the store. This became for Alex a key example of just what personal values are and how they function in a person's life. Your values are not what you say they are. Your values become clear in how you live your life. Personal values only show up in behavior. They are there; they exist, even when you don't recognize them.

Alex's friendship with Ethan went south. Ethan's behavior in the store that day demonstrated that he was not the kind of person Alex thought he was, nor the kind of person Alex wanted to be with. Think about the young store clerk in this story. At the end of the day, she would have to make up a twenty-dollar deficit at the cash register. Ethan didn't need the money, but he stole it.

Personal values are those basic principles, ways of behavior, or basic belief tenets you would find exceptionally difficult to live without. There are many personal values. Here's a list of some of them:

Authenticity	Boldness	Curiosity
Achievement	Compassion	Determination
Adventure	Challenge	Fairness
Ambition	Citizenship	Faith
Authority	Community	Fame
Autonomy	Competency	Family
Balance	Contribution	Friendships
Beauty	Creativity	Fun

Geography/place
Growth
Happiness
Helping others
Honesty
Humor
Independence
Influence
Inner harmony
Interdependence
Justice
Kindness
Knowledge
Leadership
Learning

Legacy
Love
Loyalty
Meaningful work
Morality: right and wrong
Openness
Optimism
Peace
Personal accountability
Pleasure
Popularity
Recognition
Religion

Reputation
Respect
Responsibility
Risk
Security
Self-respect
Service and charity
Spirituality
Stability
Success
Status
Trustworthiness
Wealth
Wisdom

This list is not all-inclusive. It's meant to illustrate the large variety of possible things people can value and help you understand that different people hold different values and practice different ways of behavior. However, certain values cross national and cultural boundaries and appear to be generally accepted.

Ten Core Ethical Values That Unite Humanity

- Honesty
- Integrity
- Promise keeping
- Loyalty/fidelity
- Fairness

- Concern for others
- Respect for others
- Law abidingness
- Pursuit of excellence
- Personal accountability

Source: Dale L. Brubaker and Larry D. Coble, *The Hidden Leader: Leadership Lessons on the Potential Within* (Minneapolis: Sage, 2004).

It is important for you to understand your own personal values: what they are, what meaning they have in your life, and how they affect your behavior.

Why is this important? More than anything else you read in this book, your values are going to determine much of your future. Holding onto them, being true to them, and making sure others see them in your behavior will send the most important messages you can send to anyone, be they your spouse, significant other, child, employer, friend, mentee, casual acquaintances, or just people you come across in your day-to-day life.

It is important to know whether your personal values match the organizational values of the company or business in which you work. We will be discussing organizational values a bit later in the book, but if your values don't match your employer's, you could have a values conflict. The same holds true of your personal values and whether or not they match the values of those individuals you choose to be with in your life, in or outside of work. This means that values conflicts can arise between you and a key relationship or a good friend, a spouse, a fellow volunteer, or your children. This plays out in many different ways, for example, when one's values are shown in social and political views, behavioral characteristics, and life choices.

Here is an example. At the Institute for Ethical Leadership at Rutgers University, which Alex cofounded and where he taught, he brought in a speaker to address an audience of corporate executives. The speaker was in a senior executive sales position in an international company. He felt that he had strong values and went on to describe how he resolved a values conflict. In his company, there was an exceptional push for results, and other sales executives were providing potential and current clients with monetary gifts and other rewards for making purchases of the company's products. Of course, this was against the law. He said that the environment at the company and the fact that everyone else was breaking the law eroded his own values. He adopted the company's values over his own, and therefore, the behavior eventually put him in a jail cell for almost two years. Values conflicts are resolved by individuals holding onto the values they have and continuing to resist outside influence. One can literally reject the values one does not want or try to change the environment one is in or move into a new position or a new company. Some people will decide to compromise and accept new values. It's hard to live with a values conflict for a long time, although it is possible. The stress of constantly resisting the pressure to conform can beat you down. The executive in our true story above went on to recapture his personal values by both assisting the FBI in its investigation and lecturing on the subject of ethics in business by using his situation as an example for others.

We had one client, Andy, who was asked by his married boss to help keep the boss's affair with a fellow employee under wraps. Andy considered loyalty and honesty to be core values, and this situation required him to choose with which value he would more closely align. Andy knew that the human resources department could require corrective action for both Andy and his boss if this affair came to light. Andy chose to put loyalty before honesty and agreed to keep his boss's secret over the next several months. During this time, Andy felt miserable that he had allowed his integrity to be compromised. Values are especially tested when someone has something to lose. Andy felt pressured by his boss and worried about his job and the potential for the loss of that relationship and position.

The affair did eventually come to light, and Andy's boss was reprimanded and lost his job. Andy was also reprimanded but allowed to stay in his position. The mental anguish that Andy felt during this time was a major life lesson though, and he learned to guard his core values more closely and make decisions that more accurately reflected those values.

An example demonstrating when personal values create a conflict outside of work is found in Julian's case. He values liberal or progressive political policy, while his mother and father are diehard conservatives. All of them have strongly held values. This began to cause a problem when Julian visited his parents and the subject of politics or governmental policy arose. It was apparent that no one was going to change his or her mind. Julian and his parents decided that the only thing that they could do was to avoid conversation about these issues and to focus on the values they all held together, such as love for one another, family, and sports.

When your values are clear to you, making decisions becomes easier.

—Roy Disney

What are your personal values? And where do they come from? First, there are many contributors to your values. Your family and the significant people in your life, both relatives and friends, make a contribution. Your religious beliefs, education, and life experiences all help you to discern how your values develop and just what they are. Why is this important? It's important because when you plan to create a holistic, strategic approach for your life and career, your values will be the motor to drive you forward and to help you make the decisions about the kind of work you'll do, the kind of position you'll accept, the kind of company or organization you'll join or move away from, and the kind of person you choose to be.

So let's take a look at your personal values. Here is a brief exercise to help you to discern your personal values. To guide you, we refer you back to the list of values at the beginning of the chapter, but remember that there may be a personal value you hold that is not on the list. Also, you might start out with a fairly long list of values you hold to be important, but we would encourage you not to have more than five to eight key values at the end of the exercise. As a matter of fact, you might find that some values are contained within others. For example, if you have a personal value of helping others, this might be listed as service to others or philanthropic/charitable work. Or if you have a personal value of education, the value of learning could be a part of that. In any case, try to get down to the values that really matter to you.

Here is one example. Personal accountability is one of Alex's values. This has played out in many ways over many years. When he was the CEO of an organization, he took his own personal accountability seriously and strove mightily to achieve those things for which he was responsible. However, he also held those who worked for him accountable for the results they mutually agreed they would all produce. It was important to Alex to assure that the employees also had personal accountability. It is also the major reason why Alex has never held a group or committee accountable or allowed shared accountability between two individuals for the same expected result. The buck needs to stop with someone—certainly with him as the executive but also with those who had personal accountability to produce results in their area of responsibility. This value also carried over to his personal life in many ways. For example, Alex's two sons while in college wanted to study abroad for a semester. Alex and his wife said that they could if they found a way that would cost the same or less than studying at their home university. Their sons were personally accountable for the outcome of the situation, so they found a way, achieved the result they wanted, and were able to study abroad.

You should be able, when your list of values is completed, to see just how the values you say you hold dear have been apparent in your life. Below, list the values you hold to be most important to you, along with the reason you chose that value and where you think you picked up that value, whether from your own life experience, your church, your family, or even something you read.

My Values

My personal value	Why is this important to me?	Where does it come from?
1.		
2.		
3.		

My personal value	Why is this important to me?	Where does it come from?
4.		
5.		
6.		
7.		
8.		

You now have between five and eight personal values that are important to you. You know why you have them and some idea of where they came from. Later we will compare these values to those of the organization in which you work. For now, do you see any themes emerging here in your values that also resonate in the work you did on your interests and the things that give you joy in your life? Are these themes motivating you to look holistically at your life and career? How can we get your interests, the things that give you joy, and your personal values better aligned with the work that you do and the type of organization in which you do it?

Here are a few questions to help you in this regard. Be sure to document your responses.

- Is my current job or work feeding my interests or at least allowing time for them?

    For example, many of Melissa's students expressed concern that their demanding jobs did not provide enough time for interests outside of work.

- Is my current job or work able to provide some joy in my life?

  Alex had several clients who were going through the motions on their job, feeling that they were stuck doing work they simply did not enjoy.

- Is my current job or work supporting my personal values, or am I in conflict?

  One of our graduate students told the class of an incident in which she was asked to attract clients with gifts that would have been illegal.

In addition to aligning interests, joy, and values at work, let's focus also on alignment outside of work.

- Are my personal relationships enhancing or eroding my interests?

  Some clients noted that family relationships or a significant other supported their efforts to follow their interests, while others felt they were being discouraged.

- Do my family members and friends share my values?

  A graduate student noted that some classmates wanted to socialize in the evening to a great extent. He needed to move away from this particular group since it was beginning to impact his ability to get coursework done. Education was more important to him than social interaction.

- Do I lead a life that includes laughter and joy?

  One client told a story about the weekend bike rides he had with friends. The group would kid one another, tell jokes, and laugh a lot. The client expressed how important these happy and good feelings were in his life.

By noting where your interests, joy, and values align, you begin to paint the picture of self-satisfaction or happiness that you desire. In the chart on the following page, we want to help you to do that. You will see an example of an interest that when engaged in provides joy and also is an outlet for the exercise of your personal values. An individual could have a keen interest in working with others in developing new programs at work. That work, when successful, provides this person with a great deal of joy, a real sense of achievement. At the same time, the individual loves to create and to learn, which are two important values to her. Therefore, by following a particular interest, the result is joy for the individual and an exercise of personal values. We have drawn this out in the box below and added two examples. Take a moment to list the combination of interests, joy, and values that you see in your life. These connections, between interests, joy, and values, help to form the threads of support for the life you choose to build.

The Integration of My Interests, Joy, and Values

Interests supported at work or home	Potential for joy at work or home	Values supported at work or home or lack thereof
1. Creating a new program at work with others	Leading a successful team	Learning or creating
2. Bike riding with children	Family time together	Love of family

What lessons have come to mind as you have been thinking about your personal values? List them in the box below.

What Have I Learned by Exploring My Personal Values?

_____

_____

_____

_____

_____

_____

_____

_____

To develop some ideas to consider for your action plan, here are a few more questions to consider.

- Are there any changes at home or work that I need to make to better align my values?
- Can I increase the joy in my life within my current relationships?
- Does my behavior reflect my stated values?

Ideas for My Action Plan

1. _____

2. _____

3. _____

4. _____

Each of us possesses a moral GPS, a compass or conscience
programmed by parents, teachers, coaches, grandparents, clergy,
friends, and peers. The compass is an integral part of our being.
It continues to differentiate between proper and improper
behavior until the day we die.

—Bill George, *True North*

You have now done some really good work focused on your interests, the joy in your life, and your personal values. Each of these areas is at the core of who you are. They energize and motivate you and are seen in your behavior. This means that everyone you have a relationship with can see how you represent the values and interests you hold. In chapter 4, we will review the importance of the relationships in your life and how those relationships can either help or hinder you from moving to your career and life goals.

Relationships

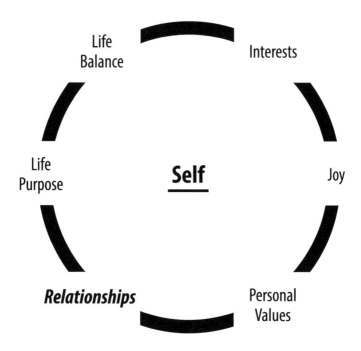

Life
Balance

Interests

Life
Purpose

Self

Joy

Relationships

Personal
Values

This chapter focuses on the key relationships in your life, their importance, and how they can help you to gain unvarnished feedback on your
decisions and plans. The chapter also includes advice about relationships
in general that can either help or hinder you in building a fulfilling life.

Key Relationships

Do you have any key relationships in your life? A key relationship is a highly important connection to an individual with whom you can share your innermost thoughts and plans, whether about your life or career. A person serving this function in your life, when asked, would provide advice and counsel on any problem or decision with which you needed help. This person would tell you what you need to hear, even if you didn't want to hear it. These individuals care about you, they seem to understand you, and they want the best for you and your future.

Richard wanted to change jobs. He didn't get along very well with his boss. One evening he came home and, in a discussion with his wife, Sarah, let her know his feelings. He told her he wanted to quit and go to another company. Sarah asked him if he had approached his boss and described to the boss why he was feeling the way he was feeling. Richard said that he had not. Sarah pressed further, noting that they had a lot to risk if he just quit, including a home, education of two children, and a good lifestyle. She suggested that before he just severed his relationship with the company, he try to salvage his relationship with his supervisor first and perhaps not have to go through the significant change required by a job search and a new position. It was good advice. Richard approached his boss and had a conversation with him that resulted in a change in their working relationship. However, six months later, his manager's behavior reverted back to its old ways, and both Sarah and Richard knew that a job change for Richard was going to be the better solution. Rather than outright quitting, Richard developed a job search that would smoothly transition him to a new employer without loss of compensation or benefits.

Sarah is a key relationship in Richard's life. She provided Richard with straightforward advice. And even though that advice only proved initially helpful, the process of talking things through helped both Richard and Sarah recognize what had to be done to get Richard closer to being happier in his work.

When addressing larger groups, Alex has always asked the audience whether they have a key relationship in their lives. He has found that although there are some individuals who do not have any key relationships, most people do have at least one.

If you are a person who does not have a key relationship in your life at all, and it is hard for you to recognize anyone special in your family or among your friends, you do have some work to do. While the well-known statement "no man is an island" holds true, some of us behave as if we are an island. We have difficulty sharing our concerns or innermost thoughts with another human being. This can be a real downside for individuals throughout their lives if sharing and seeking honest advice from another person does not seem possible. So what does one do about this lack of real connection? It is extremely important for you to examine the relationships you do have, to determine if any of them can be developed into a key relationship. If that possibility exists, then you need to focus on building up the elements of your relationship with this person. Are you willing to put time into the relationship? Can you open up to this person by sharing your thoughts with no expectation of getting anything back? Do you care enough about this person to be his or her key relationship? Are you willing to accept advice and counsel? If these and other similar questions can be responded to affirmatively, you have a good chance of developing your current relationship with this person into a key relationship. We recommend that you take the steps to do so.

You may discover that you don't have anyone in your life that you can develop into a key relationship. Or you may be one of those individuals who feel that they really don't need or want such a relationship. Can you be successful without a key relationship? Of course. However, our experience in coaching individuals informs us that a key relationship is much like a valuable resource—one that can potentially bring knowledge, clarity, and a different point of view to specific situations. That's why our recommendation is to put some time and effort into developing such a relationship. But if you don't, it's not the end of the world. Remember, you can also work with a mentor or life coach to gain objective and independent feedback.

In Alex's family, his wife and sons are key relationships for him. Alex also has a few business associates and one personal friend to whom he can turn for unvarnished advice. These are relationships that have been developed over time. They are people with whom Alex has shared thoughts about his life and career. They are honest with him about what they think. If they think he plans to do something that doesn't seem to make sense, they tell him. If they think he's on a good track, they encourage him. Family, work associates, and friends all provide a means to an end in building a solid, trusting relationship. For those of you without such a relationship, we encourage you to start the process and take the time, effort, and thought it takes to gain such a relationship. Having the advice and feedback is worth it when you try to make the best decisions for your life.

Keep away from people who try to belittle your ambitions. Small people always do that, but the really great make you feel that you, too, can become great.

—Mark Twain

For those of you who already have at least one key relationship, please write the names below and explain why or how these people fill this role in your life.

My Key Relationship(s)

Relationship(s)	Why Is This a Key Relationship?

You are in good shape. Having at least one such meaningful relationship can create for you an environment in which your life and career plan is enhanced by the insight and support provided by your key relationships.

At the conclusion of the development of your life and career plan, you should share that plan with one or more of your key relationships. Their feedback can help you discern if you are on the right path. In some cases, it may cause you to make adjustments in your plan. Sometimes a key relationship can become a mentor for life. This closeness can allow you to feel safe and comfortable sharing with another human being the approach you intend to take to move ahead with your life plan, knowing the person has only your best interest at heart.

Madison, out of college for ten years and well into her career, started feeling that the approach she was taking toward her future was aimless. She sought help from Juliana, a good friend whom she trusted. During their discussions, Madison described feeling that she was not interested in marriage or having a family and stated that she wanted to focus on her career. Juliana responded by describing how she thought Madison was extremely close to her brothers and sisters and her parents and said that it was a surprise to hear that Madison wasn't interested in a family of her own. After several conversations with Juliana that were focused on Madison's values and her career desires, a significant change began to emerge. Six months later, Madison found herself in a relationship with someone she really cared for. She also received a promotion at work and had substantially more responsibility. In time, and through conversations with Juliana, Madison began to integrate a new view of her future—marriage was now desired, especially with someone who understood that Madison wanted and needed a vibrant and important career. The question of whether to start a family was not as closed as it had been; it was now open to discussion with her fiancé. Juliana, through her care and concern for Madison, had challenged Madison's thoughts about her life. In the end, Madison discovered a way to merge a robust career with building a new family.

When talking with a key relationship and asking for feedback, it is important not to make judgments about and reject out of hand the advice you are getting. These sharing sessions are a time for you to listen, take notes, and integrate the thinking you are hearing into your own thoughts. You can include or exclude those thoughts in your plans later. Thank your key relationship for taking the time to talk with you, and do the person the honor of listening to what he or she suggests, even if you do not ultimately integrate it into your plan. This won't be the last time that you will have the opportunity to gain from the relationship. Madison did not have to accept Juliana's comments about family and work integration. But she was courteous in listening and heard something that caused her to think differently.

For those of you who have at least one key relationship, it's not too early to start telling the person about the life and career planning process you're going through. For example, as we are writing this book, Alex is also coaching a client, Brad, who is a CEO with several key relationships. After each coaching session, Brad shares the documentation with his most important key relationship, his spouse. Brad receives feedback and at times will bring it into his next coaching session. Sometimes it causes changes to his plan; other times it does not. For him, the important thing is that his thoughts and plans are being shared in a very intimate way and that he knows the feedback he is getting is unvarnished. One very important result of Brad's discussions with his spouse was their agreement on when each of them would retire from their high-powered positions. Another benefit for Brad was that his spouse expected updates periodically, and if she didn't get them, she asked for the status of his planning process.

Hannah had a key relationship with a sister. She waited until her life and career plan was completed, then sat down for a long afternoon with her sister to go over it and gain the advice that she wanted. George shared his plan development on an ongoing basis with both his wife and his adult son, who were his key relationships. This was an important thing to do since in his case, decisions about taking a job in another state, selling their home, and preparing financial plans were all on the table. George wanted to make sure that his relationships were not going to be surprised by his decision-making. And he wanted to be sure to involve them in some of the decision-making as well.

Hannah and George approached their planning and their key relationships differently. There is no set formula for using a key relationship as a resource. You choose where, when, and how to do so. The settings can be different, and the sharing can take different forms. For example, one person might orally describe his plan to his key relationship, while another could give a written document to her key relationship for review. Do what's right and comfortable for you.

To summarize, if you don't have a key relationship, try to develop at least one. If you do have key relationships, think about whom they are with and why these particular people are your key relationships. Develop a process for sharing your life and career plan with these people, either on an ongoing basis or when your plan is fully developed.

Key relationships require the capacity to build trust. Trust in a relationship creates a feeling of safety. Safety allows for personal sharing. The sharer understands that he or she can trust the relationship and therefore can be open and transparent in a dialogue. The receiver in the relationship understands that trust is the basis for the relationship and therefore knows that the sharer is vulnerable, and the receiver would never do anything to break confidence or to hurt the person who is sharing. Such a relationship should propel you, the sharer, toward your best life.

Negative Relationships

It's also important to recognize that relationships can hinder an individual's progress toward his or her best life. These are negative or toxic relationships; they poison the efforts of an individual from moving in a positive direction.

Brian was a good guy who found he was constantly dealing with criticism from his older brother, Michael. Brian would periodically approach Michael for advice on various issues impacting his life. Michael consistently found negative aspects in Brian's decision-making or behavior. He did not reinforce or applaud Brian's positive behavior or decisions. He dwelled on the negative. This really bothered Brian. What should he do? What would you do?

Lanesha was working for a large company in customer relations and was supervised by Greg. Whenever Lanesha received feedback from Greg, there was always a hint of sexual overtone in his response. This made her very uncomfortable. She wasn't quite sure what to do about it because she needed her job. What should Lanesha do? What would you do?

In each of these instances and many others that you can think of, we have an individual attempting to move forward in his or her life but hitting a roadblock in the form of a negative or toxic relationship. You might even think of instances when one person in a married couple is toxic for the other person, or you might have a close family member who constantly argues with you or perhaps a son or daughter who engages in your life in uncomfortable ways. Whether it's a friend, family member, boss, or spouse doesn't matter. What matters is that this frustration in the relationship makes you feel negative, nontrusting of the individual, and concerned that you cannot share your true feelings or innermost thoughts.

Just as a positive key relationship can help you move ahead to your best life, a negative or toxic relationship can prevent you from making progress. Each negative or toxic relationship is different and should be dealt with on its own. For example, in the case noted earlier, Brian could approach his brother directly, which we know takes some courage. He could express his feelings and determine whether that type of discussion will change his brother's behavior. If it doesn't, Brian may find himself deciding that it would be best not to discuss important details of his life with his brother and to keep their relationship on a more informal basis.

Lanesha has several options. She can take a risk and let Greg know that his behavior is making her uncomfortable. The risk is that Greg may accept this information in a very negative way, which could place her job in jeopardy. Lanesha could also seek advice from her human resources department. This too has some risk since in any large organization the human resources department is required to investigate sexual harassment. If Lanesha doesn't want to assume either of these risks, there is a third choice that she would have to assess the risk for, namely, seeking another position within or outside her company.

Some toxic relationships are dealt with early in their development because the individuals involved reach a level of discomfort with each other before the relationship is completely embedded in their lives. However, other toxic relationships can last for years. They can explode, end up in divorce, family arguments, loss of job, or worse. Or a toxic relationship can achieve resolution when faced head-on. Each individual responsible for oneself has to make these decisions. Our advice is don't delay. Refuse to live with a relationship that makes you feel bad, turns you off, creates negative energy for you, and doesn't help move you along to your best life. You can seek the advice and help of one of your positive key relationships. You can seek guidance from a mentor or coach. Living with a negative or toxic relationship should not be an option.

Positive Relationships

Everyone needs some positive relationships in his or her life. These are not key relationships as described earlier. Instead they are relationships that are able to bring some lightness and color into your life. They are the family members whom you always look forward to seeing. They are the friends with whom you love to travel. They are the men and women who share your interests. They are the kind of people who have values that align with yours. They are your advisers and supporters at work. They are your friendly neighbors.

Positive relationships can occur through happenstance. But it's more likely that they are developed over time and with attention. Maurice built friendships by starting a sports night with the men in his neighborhood. He invited them to his home to watch key games in various sports depending on the interests of his neighbors. Kahlil wanted very much to spend more time with his children and grandchildren. He developed a twice-per-year weekend vacation for the entire family, which led to enjoyment and greater bonding. Florence wanted to get closer to her friends at work. She started a book club by circulating a list of current books and asking her coworkers to rate the books they might like to read and discuss. Danielle was a widow and came into contact with three other widows living in her town. She decided to create a stronger relationship by asking if they might like to have dinner and a movie together once a month.

You have examples in your life of positive relationships. You may even be working on building some right now. Its important to recognize that other people can shed light on our lives and bring color into it. They represent fun and friendship; enjoyable times together; family support; beach, gym, or running buddies; or whatever other form these relationships fit into your life.

Individuals with robust relationships maximize their chance for happiness. It's not easy to be a workaholic if you know you have to play tennis twice a week with Laura. It's harder to be alone watching television for hours when Paul expects you to have lunch with him at least once a week. A cure for feeling old occurs when you get out to watch your grandchildren play soccer, baseball, or football. Relationships push you outside of yourself. They require solid interaction between human beings. Relationships also vary in their intensity. The key is to have enough of them to bring variety and interest into your life.

What's the status of your relationships? Will some work be required as a part of your plan? What lessons have come to mind as you have been thinking about your relationships? List them in the box below.

What Have I Learned by Exploring My Relationships?

_____

_____

_____

_____

_____

_____

_____

To help you to strengthen the relationships in your life, noted below are the three areas discussed in this chapter and the opportunity to think about what positive steps you might take to improve in each of these areas.

Ideas for My Action Plan Regarding My Key Relationships

1. _____

2. _____

3. _____

Ideas for My Action Plan Regarding My Positive Relationships

1. _____

2. _____

3. _____

Ideas for My Action Plan Regarding My Negative or Toxic Relationships

1. _____

2. _____

3. _____

A friend is one that knows you as you are, understands where you have been, accepts what you have become and still gently allows you to grow.

—William Shakespeare

In chapter 5, we'll be looking at your life's mission or purpose. Your purpose will be informed by your key relationships and the work that you have already done on your interests, joy, and personal values.

As we were writing this book, Senator John McCain passed away. We believe that Senator McCain saw his mission as service to his country. This was demonstrated when as a prisoner of war he refused to be repatriated because he knew that the North Vietnamese would use it as a propaganda ploy. However, he was also a politician, and there were times he voted against his party's position because he thought it was best for the country. It was easy to discern Senator McCain's mission because it combined his interests, his personal values, his relationships, and those things that provided joy to what he described as a fulfilling and happy life.

Now it's time to work on your purpose or mission.

CHAPTER 5

Life Purpose

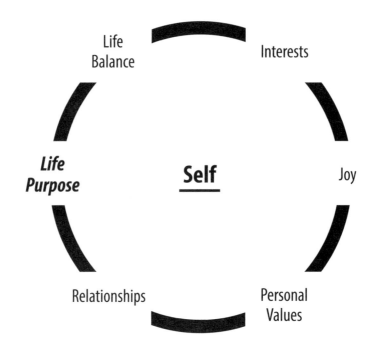

This chapter focuses on some deep questions such as, Why am I here? Who am I? Does my life have meaning? The purpose of our work in this chapter is to develop a personal mission statement.

A number of years ago Alex had the opportunity to work with Frances Hesselbein, the CEO of the Girl Scouts of America, who had been named as the best executive leader in the United States in business, nonprofit, or government fields. She talked about the need that people have for a hope beyond the change experienced in their daily lives. She said that the need was for an anchor, a purpose, which provided meaning for their life and their work. We believe everyone needs this, but few people take the time to think about it and to provide that meaning for themselves.

When teaching or coaching individuals, we ask that they write a statement that describes their life's purpose. For most people, this is not an easy exercise. It requires thinking about all the dimensions of your life, your relationships, your work, your personal motivations, and in some sense your spiritual or humanistic beliefs. A personal mission statement offers clarity and gives you a sense of purpose. It helps define who you are and how you will live. Frankly, it's much easier to write a description of a job you want than to answer the question Why am I here?

So what is your life's mission or purpose? It might help if we provided an example of Alex's own thinking about this. Some people might say that a life's mission or purpose doesn't change. However, Alex doesn't belong to that school of thinking. For example, when he was younger and getting started in his career, with two young children, his life's purpose was oriented toward career achievement and making a contribution to his family. Now he finds his life's purpose to be different in orientation, but it also includes the old stated purpose as well. Alex's thinking has broadened, and his life experience has provided a rich reservoir that helps him to make better sense of his life and to have a greater understanding of its meaning and to what he is committed.

For the past twenty years, Alex's personal mission statement has been "to help individuals and organizations to become what they seek to become while encouraging them to discern and understand their full potential and to have the courage to strive toward that potential." As you can see, he still wants to have a meaningful career. He wants to help the people in his family as well as those in his work life. The language he uses in his mission statement is general enough to cover both his personal and work life. This plays out in different ways. When working with an organization, Alex wants to be sure that he helps the leaders of that organization to see the potential the organization has and to develop appropriate plans to achieve that potential. When his daughters-in-law, sons, or grandchildren seek his advice, he provides encouragement, asks important questions, and pushes them toward fulfilling their own personal goals. He does the same thing for all of his clients. His mission resonates for him; it strikes a chord that nurtures his interests, gives him joy, deploys his values, and helps him to understand why he was placed in this world.

A mission statement is not something you write overnight. . . .
But fundamentally, your mission statement becomes your constitution,
the solid expression of your vision and values. It becomes the
criterion by which you measure everything else in your life.

—Stephen Covey, *The Seven Habits of Highly Effective People*

Now, Alex's mission or purpose statement is rather short. However, while working with students, managers, and executives, we have seen mission statements that are one, two, or three paragraphs long or even longer. The length of the statement doesn't matter. What matters is that it provides you the descriptive meaning of your life, the mission that you are deploying, and resonates with you and responds to the questions Who am I? and Why am I here?

When Melissa was midcareer, she worked with a coach to define her life's purpose. Her purpose statement is, "I bring people together in harmony." A personal example in her life was when she married a man with three children. Melissa has two children of her own, and it was a second marriage for them both. At the time of her marriage, the five children were in late teenage or early adult stages of their lives. It was important to Melissa that the new family function as a cohesive unit as much as possible, and she focused her energy and efforts toward creating a harmonious environment where all could develop and thrive. Today, the integrated family enjoys their time together, and each member feels valued as an individual and member of the larger group.

At work, Melissa teaches life and career planning at Rutgers University through the Institute for Ethical Leadership. The group of individuals she teaches works together to better understand their values, interests, relationships, and life purpose. She sets up a harmonious environment to facilitate this important introspective work. These sessions are not free of argument or divisiveness, but she strives for understanding and common ground as well as acceptance of difference.

Below are some prompts to get you started on developing your own purpose or mission statement.

My Purpose or Mission

This is who I am:

(Describe the many facets of you and your life—what kind of person are you?)

_____

_____

_____

_____

_____

This is why I am here:

(What is your purpose in life? It helps define who you are and how you will live.)

_____

_____

_____

_____

This is how my life takes on meaning:

(What is most important to you? This can be experiences, feelings, people, or values.)

_____

_____

_____

_____

This is to what I am committed:

(What do you consider nonnegotiable in your life? What do you always show up for? What do you refuse to abandon?)

_____

_____

_____

_____

This is how I want to live my life:

(Put all these things together to form a picture of how you want your life to look at its best.)

_____

_____

_____

_____

_____

Some examples of mission statements from some prominent people as noted in _Forbes_ magazine include the following:[1]

To serve as a leader, live a balanced life, and apply ethical principles to make a significant difference.

—Denise Morrison, CEO of Campbell Soup Company

To be a teacher. And to be known for inspiring my students to be more than they thought they could be.

—Oprah Winfrey, founder of OWN: The Oprah Winfrey Network

To have fun in [my] journey through life and learn from [my] mistakes.

—Sir Richard Branson, founder of the Virgin Group

To use my gifts of intelligence, charisma, and serial optimism to cultivate the self-worth and net-worth of women around the world.
—Amanda Steinberg, founder of Dailyworth.com

Here are examples of mission statements developed by individuals we have coached or who have attended our seminars:

To be true to my faith by being honest in all of my dealings with others. To deploy my faith in advising and helping others. To be productive and to make a contribution to my community.

To love and support my family. To help my children to grow into thoughtful and generous human beings. To have a successful career to support my family's lifestyle.

To progress in my career in the nonprofit field so that arts organizations remain vibrant and a part of our civil society. In doing this, mentor and develop individuals who will share in this mission.

To be my best self everyday so I live a quality life that brings joy and prosperity to me, and joy to the lives of my friends and loved ones.

My purpose in life is to grow my accounting and auditing practice so clients perceive it as a high-quality operation while providing substantial income for my family and me. I intend to coach a younger generation in this business so that I can build a bridge to my retirement by working on a reduced basis over several years. I will also volunteer and serve on boards in my community in order to give back.

My mission in life is to have a career that is both enjoyable and helps me to earn a high level of compensation that will support a very comfortable lifestyle for my husband and me. My work will include mentoring and supporting individuals in my business so that they grow and my business grows. I will intentionally choose volunteer assignments in organizations that support my personal and business interests. I will build a life that allows me to retire at age sixty and focus on my volunteer interests.

My mission in life is to provide a safe haven for homeless dogs. I work to support my basic needs and a lifestyle I enjoy while raising funds to operate a facility that provides care and shelter for local dogs. This brings me great joy and deep satisfaction as I care for these animals' needs. I choose to serve my community and these dogs because I have a deep faith in the bond that exists between human beings, animals, and our earth. I also help to find permanent homes for these dogs, which in turn creates for many families a lifelong relationship and love. I not only use the funds that I raise to support the dogs; I have a program to present information on the subject of caring for and loving dogs, which is provided to elementary schools.

Every life is a profession of faith, and exercises an inevitable and silent propaganda. . . . Every man's conduct is an unspoken sermon that is forever preaching to others.

—Henri F. Amiel, Swiss moral philosopher, poet, and critic

Now that you have thought a bit about your purpose in life and seen how other people have drafted their mission statements, let's try a first draft.

My Purpose Statement

_____

_____

_____

_____

_____

_____

_____

_____

_____

_____

_____

_____

When reading your purpose statement, does it tell you why you are here? Does it describe the essence of your life and how it will be used? Does it reflect your values? If you can say yes to these questions, you have done a great job. If your purpose statement doesn't feel perfect, it's okay. For help, go back and look at your responses to the previous chapters in the book and later return to your purpose statement after you complete the next chapters and determine if changes would be helpful. You should have a statement that you really like for inclusion in your life and career planning process.

What practical effect can your purpose statement have in building your life? José had engaged in a job search for nearly four months. He was successful in that he now had two job offers to be considered. He had diligently completed a life and career plan and began to compare that plan to the two job offers: What would each job mean to his relationships, values, life balance, and so forth? Most important was whether one job or the other was going to fit in with his life's purpose. When comparing his purpose statement to each of the positions, it became easier for José to make his decision. The positions were comparable with regard to role, compensation, and future development. One of them, however, would provide more meaning and purpose to his life. His decision was made.

Vikram and Julie met in college. They lost contact with each other for more than ten years but later met at a party in New York City. They began to date and became interested in being with each other, so much so that their discussions soon began to focus on the potential for a life together. Julie did not have a purpose statement for her life, nor had she thought much about the integration of her life and career. Vikram, on the other hand, had spent considerable time thinking about who he was and where he was going. He decided to share his purpose statement with Julie. It immediately caused them to have to explore how they might live together, recognizing Vikram's desire to engage in a global business that would bring him home to India on a frequent basis. This in turn made Julie consider whether her life's purpose could be compatible with Vikram's.

Purpose statements can be quite powerful in motivating a person toward one's specific life vision. The statement can help with decision-making in all aspects of one's life. As Frances Hesselbein has observed, a well-thought-out statement provides an anchor in life's sea of change.

We're sure that thinking about your purpose statement created some learning for you. What were those lessons? List them in the box below.

What Have I Learned by Exploring My Life Purpose?

_____

_____

_____

_____

_____

_____

_____

_____

_____

_____

What you learned in this chapter about your mission or purpose in life should provide you with some ideas for actions in your life and career plan. Note them on the following page.

Ideas for My Action Plan

1. _____

2. _____

3. _____

4. _____

As noted earlier in this chapter, your mission or purpose may or may not change at some future point in your life. It could be that changes in your environment, both small and large, might have an impact on how you see your life's purpose. Because of that, reviewing your mission should be a part of the review of your life and career plan every two years or when some major life event occurs. Aligning all of the parts of your life and career plan with your purpose is like fitting the pieces of a puzzle together. It provides the opportunity to make your life better and to help you feel good about your place in the world. Let your purpose strengthen your resolve, help you to make decisions, and bring you a level of comfort.

Just how do I keep everyone, including myself, on track and motivated
through each long year—all for one long night's big splash?
The answer is basic and simple: through an unwavering
and uncompromising focus on . . . mission.

—Eric Harvey, David Cottrell, Al Lucia, and Mike Hourigan,
The Leadership Secrets of Santa Claus

One subject consistently comes up in our seminars and when we coach individuals: life balance. That is, how does one live a life that is holistic, incorporating work, interests, and relationships so that harmony is a product of our living? You will need to address your life balance as a part of your life and career plan. We will cover that in chapter 6.

CHAPTER 6

Life Balance

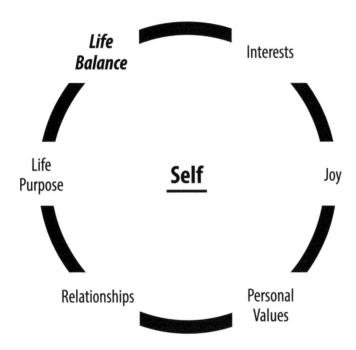

This chapter focuses on helping you to understand your current life balance and whether some changes need to be made and how to go about making those changes.

"My life is out of balance."

"I'm a workaholic and I can't seem to have a more balanced life."

"It's really hard for me to spend time with family, do my work, and find time for myself."

"This job is killing me. I'm losing parts of my life every day."

"I'm retired, and I have plenty of time on my hands. I just wish I knew how to use it."

Sound familiar? Each one of us has a limited amount of time every day, every month, every year. Your life is actually spent in the minutes, hours, and days that belong to you until they are gone. How and where you spend that time is up to you. However, it's greatly influenced by a number of things, including the organization you work for, the needs of your family, your own needs, your health, your financial situation, and the strength of your relationships, among other things.

Never get so busy making a living that you forget to make a life.

—Dolly Parton

In both the coaching and seminars in which we're engaged, individuals often report that they have an unbalanced life. Many of them are stuck. Their jobs demand too much, their family needs are great, or their finances are limited. Even individuals with substantial incomes and demanding jobs complain about life balance: not being able to use that income effectively to gain a better lifestyle. You can almost hear them saying, "I can't get out of my own way." In some sense, the words "life balance" describe what we are talking about, but that phrase is inadequate. That's because we are not saying that 20 percent of your life should be spent here and 15 percent here and 30 percent there. What we mean by "life balance" is that your life is holistic, interconnected, free flowing, and hopefully, personally rewarding. We all know that there will be some twelve-hour days at work, but if we're working like that all of the time, we are in trouble. We also know that for most people it isn't fun to spend time on our finances, but if we don't, we will never get them straightened out. We think our relationships with our friends, significant others, or children draw us away from the work we need to do, and yet we would be hard-pressed to have the life we want without those relationships. What to do?

Below is a chart. On the left side are some common things that people spend time on. Please add whatever you like to the list on the left. On the right, put in the percentage of time that you spend on each area. The total should amount to 100 percent of your time. Do that now.

How I Spend My Time

Activity	Average % of time spent daily	Average % of time spent weekly
Work		
Family activities		
Recreational pursuits		
Sleep		
Time with friends / significant others		
Learning		
Exercising		

Do your responses reflect a typical day or week in your life? If not, adjust them. Once your chart looks right to you, what else can you glean from it? Does anything leap out at you? Using the work you've already done on your plan, does it appear that you spend your life in a way that mirrors your interests, what gives you joy, your personal values, your relationships, and meaningful and important work? If necessary, go back to the previous chapters to refresh yourself on your answers about what you value. If the way you spend your life doesn't reflect the things that are important to you, why not? Are your percentages just a little out of balance? Or do you have a lot of work to do to move yourself in a positive direction? Healthy individuals and healthy leaders should have multiple sources of satisfaction in their lives. The things that can provide satisfaction in your life might come from an interest such as reading, an action such as volunteering, or just being with family and friends. Certain aspects of one's work can provide satisfaction as well. The Menninger Foundation reports the following:

- The best adjusted people have multiple sources of gratification.
- They respect others as individuals.
- They are flexible.
- They accept their limitations and assets.
- They are productive and active.[1]

So how do you compare with these study results?

- What are your sources of gratification?
- Do you demonstrate respect for other individuals regardless of their station in life?
- How flexible are you?
- Do you know what your limitations and assets are?
- How active and productive are you?

For purposes of inspiration, think about someone in your life or in public life that you believe exemplifies a happy and healthy person. Take a moment to describe his or her attributes and attitudes in the space below. Although one can never fully understand another person's life and what goes on behind closed doors, it is possible for you to see in the demeanor and behavior of someone certain characteristics that make you say, "I would like to be more like that."

You will never feel truly satisfied by work until you are satisfied by life.
—Heather Schuck, *The Working Mom Manifesto*

Someone You Know Who Appears to Be a Happy and Healthy Person

Name:

_____

Attributes and attitudes:

_____

_____

_____

_____

_____

_____

If we know what we think makes a happy and healthy person and we have in our sights people who appear to live such a life, it seems the next question should be, "How do I get there?"

Rebecca Webber notes in an article in *Psychology Today*,

Social comparison theory was first put forth in 1954 by psychologist Leon Festinger, who hypothesized that we make comparisons as a way of evaluating ourselves. At its root, the impulse is connected to the instant judgments we make of other people. "Inevitably, we relate information about others to ourselves," says Thomas Mussweiler, a professor of organizational behavior at London Business School. "It's one of the most basic ways we develop an understanding of who we are, what we're good at, and what we're not so good at." . . . Self-improvement occurs when an upward comparison inspires us to try harder. Self-enhancement can take place when we note our similarities to someone superior. . . . As we age, we're more likely to evaluate ourselves against the yardstick of our own past rather than the present state of others.[2]

Having a balanced life doesn't happen by accident. It requires an intentional approach toward one's life, aimed at achieving a comfort level that an individual desires in all areas that matter to him or her. It's next to impossible to move immediately from being a workaholic to having a well-balanced life. Moving in a positive direction is a step-by-step process. It requires a personal commitment. For example, Ken explained that his job required twelve- to fourteen-hour days to get the work done. Over time, he committed to a work reduction of one hour at a time until he reached the point where he, his employer, and his coworkers understood how much he was willing to invest in his job and what he needed outside of work to be a happy and healthy individual.

When an individual starts to take action toward balancing one's life, there is an inherent risk. The risk can be in the form of potentially losing a job. In Ken's example, the employer might have thought that reducing his work hours was also a reduction in commitment to the company and job. Ken might have been classified as not a team player, not contributing all that he could to getting the work done. Taking another risk could lead to a stressed marriage. Sylvia wants Larry to go antiquing with her on weekends, but Larry would rather play softball with the guys. Somehow he has to support his own interest at the risk of upsetting Sylvia.

In these examples, Ken, Sylvia, and Larry might consider what would minimize risk in their situations. In Ken's case, having a conversation with his supervisor to describe his intent as well as his commitment to the job would be helpful. Sylvia and Larry could agree that softball is the focus in spring and summer while antiquing is the focus in fall and winter.

At times, it may be important to ask for help. This can be done at work or at home with a key relationship, a friend, or an associate. It requires naming the thing that is preventing you from moving toward a more balanced life and then constructing a set of action steps that moves you in a more positive direction.

Whenever Alex took on a new position, he would have a conversation with his wife about the fact that his learning curve would be steep and that he would need to work longer hours than normal, at least for a period of time. He would ask for her understanding for six or seven months. At the end of that time, he would commit to a more normal workday and spending more time with her and at home. So he would work very hard for those first six months, knowing that he had a commitment to move toward a saner work-life balance after that.

There were times when our clients told us that they simply did not have the opportunity to make the kinds of decisions that would rescue them from unhealthy situations. Perhaps they had a boss who provided little understanding of how overworked they were, or their position required more work than any one person could do, or the staffing in the area in which they worked left it greatly underresourced.

In some cases, individuals can create greater synergy and interdependence in their current situation, little by little, by using their interests, their relationships, or their passions to create balance among the various aspects of their life. Sometimes that's not possible. Usually this is apparent in people who have reached the end of their rope in their present circumstances and are not committed to putting in the work to change where they are but instead want a completely new work environment. So you can change what you do and how you react within your current environment, or you can change the environment at work or at home to support what you actually need. Or you can move to a totally new environment to get what you want and create the balance you are missing in your life.

You won't really know whether you can change your own behavior until you start making incremental changes and notice that they are working. You can't change your current work or home environment unless you ask for what you want where you are. This takes courage, because it might cause some risk at work or at home. Completely changing your environment at home or at work is a more drastic solution that should only be considered when the first two things, that is, gradually changing yourself or your current environment, don't work.

Roberto's life balance was quite comfortable for him for a long time. However, his two sons soon began to grow their own families. He now had two grandchildren, which reprioritized his interests, leading to a change in his life balance. He and his wife, Ruthanne, decided that they could help their children more by caring for their grandchildren for as many as four days a week. His sons were not able to afford the high cost of day care for their children. This new allotment of time took time away from Roberto's hobbies, which included woodworking and automobile restoration. Roberto and Ruthanne made a conscious decision to change their priorities—one that they truly desired, that was driven by their values, and that positioned them to build a close relationship with their grandchildren.

Defining what a balanced life looks like for you is important. The holistic combinations of interests, passions, family, work, and volunteerism are different for different people. A retiree is likely to focus more on interests and passion than on work. A young adult might want to build a career first and to move ahead in that career. A mature individual might have a family, a home, and hobbies as well as work to be balanced in a way that meets his or her needs. What would meet your needs right now? Can you discern how you might spend your time over the course of a day or a week to produce the comfort level you would like to have in your life's balance? Take a look at the chart that you completed at the beginning of this chapter. It denotes where you're spending your time now. How would you rather spend that time? What changes would you like to make?

Let's take some time to imagine and write about your own best life as it relates to your life balance. So far, you've thought about an individual to keep in mind for inspiration, you've been given some examples of life balance situations, and you also know where you are currently spending your time. It may help if you write a paragraph or two describing your life when your life balance is in a positive state.

Here is an example from someone we know.

I am in balance when:

- I protect my boundaries and stay focused on work projects at work and focused on my personal life at home.
- I prioritize work demands and don't let procrastination hinder forward progress.
- I eat and drink in a way that respects my body allowing myself to splurge about 10% of the time because this also represents balance to me.
- I make time to exercise vigorously at least four times a week because this keeps me feeling my best.
- I keep promises I have made to people who are important to me and keep promises to myself as well.
- My finances are in order and I am following my financial plan.
- I avoid spending time on things that don't support my goals and interests, like binge watching a program that is only moderately interesting.
- I regularly express gratitude for the wonderful people in my life, for my health, and for the blessings and opportunities that come my way every day.

When My Life Is in Balance and in a Positive State, It Looks like This

_____

_____

_____

_____

_____

So now, based on what you have learned, indicate below how you would like to spend your time in an average day or week.

How I Would Like to Spend My Time

Activity	Average % of time spent daily	Average % of time spent weekly
Work		
Family activities		
Recreational pursuits		
Sleep		

Activity	Average % of time spent daily	Average % of time spent weekly
Time with friends / significant others		
Learning		
Exercising		
Add here anything that you added in the chart above:		

Now that we know what your life balance currently looks like and what you would like it to look like, we need to consider how we build the bridge from one to the other. This is going to require tailor-made plans and decision-making from you. You'll need to think about those areas of your life where time spent has to be reduced or eliminated and those areas where it has to be increased. You'll have to think about to whom you will need to talk—your boss, your spouse or your significant other, a friend—and you will need to think about taking action steps that are specific, measurable, attainable, realistic, and time-sensitive toward the vision you want.

You will never find time for anything. If you want time you must make it.

—Charles Buxton, English philanthropist, writer, and member of Parliament

---

As a young manager working for a large corporation, Alex enjoyed playing tennis. However, he never had much time to do so. He had small children at the time, and his weekends were spent around the house working, playing with the kids, and enjoying time with his wife. He missed playing tennis and decided he needed to find a way to play more than he had been playing. This decision required him to talk to his wife so that she understood what he planned to do. Alex began to leave work to play tennis two or three times a week with some business associates around 4:00 p.m. At 5:30, Alex would be home having dinner with the family. He lived five minutes from his office, so by 6:30 p.m., he went back to work for a while and then was home at 8:00 p.m., just in time to put the kids to bed. This gave him his comfort level. He was playing tennis two or three times a week, was having dinner with his family, had his weekends free, and got his work done. What is happening in your life that is bringing your balance out of whack, and what could be your solution?

Maria felt that she needed to find the time to exercise. Her company had just added a new gym with shower facilities, so she rearranged her schedule to be able to go to the gym at 6:00 a.m., get in a full workout, and then shower and be at her desk by 7:30 a.m. This was a small change, yet she benefited tremendously from this exercise program by getting in shape and gaining energy for the day.

When Melissa enrolled in the Rutgers Business School Executive MBA Program, she met individuals who wanted very much to complete their advanced degree and gain additional knowledge and experience for their résumés. Many of them had to approach their employer about time off, since the program required being at the university every other Friday. They negotiated the time off with their supervisors and also had to speak to their significant others about the fact that many evenings would now have to be spent on completing the work for their MBA. These highly motivated individuals needed to change the way that they spent their time and had to rebalance their lives so that they could achieve a lifetime goal.

There is no prescription that we can write for you that will make your life more balanced, but you can write one for yourself. Compare the two charts that you've filled out in this chapter, choose the area or areas in which you are willing to make an incremental or abrupt change, make a plan, and take decisive action.

The first step is to document in the space below what you have learned about your life balance.

What Have I Learned by Exploring My Life Balance?

_____

_____

_____

_____

_____

_____

_____

_____

_____

_____

Next, looking at each of the activities in your life and what you have learned, note below the actions you would like to consider including in your life and career plan. Try to put a time line on each of the actions so that when you do your plan, those actions can be included within your plan's two-year time frame.

Actions to Consider

Activity	Action to be taken	Time line
Work		
Family activities		
Recreational pursuits		
Sleep		
Time with friends / significant others		
Learning		
Exercising		
Add here anything that you added in the chart above:		

Happiness is not a matter of intensity but of balance, order, rhythm, and harmony.

—Thomas Merton, American Trappist monk, writer, theologian, mystic, poet, social activist, and scholar of comparative religion

---

We would like to leave with you a few thoughts or ideas that could be helpful.

- If you don't already, try using a monthly calendar and slotting in the times for those things that are important to you, for example, your interests, family time, time for friends, time for sports or recreation, time for hobbies. Also, slot in special activities for work, such as having lunch with a coworker.
- Think about using a follow-up system, noting in advance with a specific date an action that you will take to have influence on your life balance, for example, learning a language, taking a tennis lesson, shopping with your significant other.
- You have control over a powerful word: *no*. You have more options than you think when working or volunteering. When faced with an option, not a demand, and you can easily say no, think about your life-balance priorities and determine if a yes fits or doesn't fit.
- When faced with a seemingly unalterable life-balance situation, get help. Talk to a friend, a key relationship, or a coach.

We have just completed the first part of the model. We examined aspects of *you*. We focused on your interests, joy, values, relationships, purpose, and life balance. This first part, self-examination, isn't easy. Congratulations on completing it. In our opinion, the next part of the model is not as difficult since it focuses on things that are much more familiar to you. We can now move on to an examination of aspects of your work and career.

PART II

Work and Career

A Review of Those Aspects of Your Work and Career That Help You to Better Perform and Progress

CHAPTER 7

Personal Strengths and Development Areas

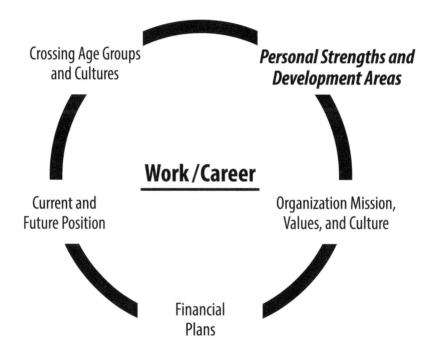

This chapter asks you to be as objective as possible in discerning your personal and professional strengths and areas requiring further development. Then you will have an opportunity to choose actions to be incorporated into your plan that will meet your development needs.

In chapter 6, we mentioned a study that was done by the Menninger Foundation. The study noted the characteristics of a happy and healthy person. One of those characteristics was the acceptance of one's limitations and assets. Individuals can't accept their limitations or assets unless they can identify them and be honest about them. What are your strengths and areas requiring personal development? How do you find out what they are if you don't already know?

First, we understand that the strengths that an individual has can dramatically change over time. For example, an ability to play a specific sport may diminish. Other strengths, like being able to lead a large number of individuals at work, might increase. Strengths, identified as areas of specific power, energy, knowledge, skill, or intensity that one embodies and can rely on, are different today than they were yesterday and could be different tomorrow. Much depends on an individual's focus on those strengths to acquire, build, or maintain them. In addition, individuals learn throughout their life, whether formally or through experience. We believe learning is lifelong; therefore, personal development is lifelong. Personal development is defined by an individual's actions, which improve awareness and self-identity and develop talents, skills, and potential. A company that Alex worked for had a motto: "The future belongs to those who prepare for it." This means that plans for your future can be better achieved if you develop the skills and abilities for who you want to become.

Knowing others is intelligence; knowing yourself is true wisdom. Mastering others is strength; mastering yourself is true power.

—Lao Tzu, *Tao Te Ching*

When approached with the question "What are your strengths at work?" some people might say things like dealing with people, financial acumen, or project management. Approached on the same basis when asked about strengths outside of work, individuals might say raising children, volunteer activities, or playing a sport. Most people are able to easily respond to these questions because they intuitively understand their strengths.

When asked, "What do you do for your personal development?" responses might be "I'm studying for an advanced degree"; "I accept rotational assignments at work"; "I read a lot about my personal interest in astronomy"; or "I'm learning to play bridge."

Alex and Melissa have coached individuals who have taken different roads to their self-development. Some were focused on education, others on seeking new job assignments or new employers, and still others on a complete change in career direction. Melissa herself moved from the for-profit world to nonprofit and then back again to for-profit. Alex chose to learn about business, nonprofit, and government by accepting positions in each of these sectors. One of our clients, Brandon, decided to go to law school after a fifteen-year career in business. Rose Marie moved from full-time work in her career as a nurse to part-time work helping to run a home health care business. Each individual wanted to learn something new and develop a new strength or skill.

Just as an individual might have savings and investments that form his or her financial capital, you have a lot of human capital in your areas of strength. Financial capital can increase through savings and investment returns. So, if you want more human capital, focus on development and build up your strengths. Be realistic when assessing the limitations that you need to overcome. Is the limitation holding you back at work, or is it something that if you overcame it, it would make your nonwork life more fulfilling? Is it a limitation that is a top priority requiring immediate attention? Or is it one that can be worked on over a longer period of time? Similarly, when thinking about the assets that you have and those that you need to acquire, some will need to be maintained now and some will need to be developed for the future. For example, if you are a manager or executive, your assets might be your ability to supervise, manage, and assess individuals. Those assets will grow as you acquire more work experience. Other assets, outside of work, such as your ability to play tennis, might diminish over time, requiring movement from playing singles to playing doubles. In other words, this kind of strategic thinking will help you to prioritize where you want to spend your time, energy, and resources and to better assure that they are being applied in areas that you choose to be your current priority.

In some cases, for example, attorneys, financial planners, and certified public accounts are required to participate in continuing education so that their knowledge is constantly updated. This could also apply to the field in which you work. Of course, anyone can plan and execute a continuing education program for himself or herself.

Just prior to Alex's thirty-fifth birthday, he reached a point where he felt that he really didn't need to have someone else's evaluation of his strengths or weaknesses. He evaluated himself on a regular basis. He knew that he had a high degree of people and management skills, but he also knew that he needed to learn more about the financials of a company. Alex felt that he had enough formal education, but he needed to focus on gaining a higher degree of technological skill and knowledge. This led him to take assignments on a rotational basis— one in accounting and another on a team to build a new computer system for the company.

Alex believed that he had reached a stage of maturity that allowed him to recognize and accept what he saw as his strengths, as well as areas of his life that needed development. This didn't mean that Alex was unwilling to accept feedback from another person about those things; it just meant that he didn't lie to himself, accepted his limitations, and planned to do something about them.

There is nothing noble in being superior to your fellow man; true nobility is being superior to your former self.

—Ernest Hemingway

Let's take a look at your personal and professional strengths. What might be one of your personal strengths? Some common examples of personal strengths include creative thinking, timeliness, personal accountability, organizational ability, sense of humor, and patience. What might be some of your professional strengths? Some common examples of professional strengths include financial acumen, people skills, teamwork, strategy development, and mentoring. How do we discern that we have these strengths and areas of development? We can be told about them by someone else—for example, a boss, colleague, spouse, or kids, We can take tests to determine if we have a high degree of emotional intelligence, good teamwork skills, or good planning skills. So if you've gotten feedback from any source or taken any kind of test or exam, you have some idea of what your areas of strength or development might be. If you're honest with yourself, you can even evaluate your own areas of strength and development from your prior experiences.

Over the past few years, Melissa recognized that she had an interest in and a need to develop her skill with social media engagement and marketing. She sought out online courses, webinars, and articles that focused in this area. She experimented with new ways of engaging with social media, shared her new knowledge with others experienced in the field, and sought feedback. Melissa was able to overcome the discomfort that she had, developed new learning, and became quite proficient in the use of social media.

In our experience, individuals can be delayed in their development because they reject the feedback they are getting from a boss or the results of a test they have taken. In other words, when confronted with this new information, their reaction is, "That's really not me." We know that it's easier for individuals to hear positive information about their strengths but more difficult to accept negative information or constructive criticism. Therefore, it's important to be open to the information received and accepting of it so that it can be used to drive you forward in a more positive direction.

We have found that clients who have a difficult time accepting constructive criticism have a very difficult time changing their behavior.

For example, in one case, Sidney repeatedly received feedback that he overcontrolled others and gave the impression that his way of accomplishing things was always the best way. It didn't matter whether coworkers or executives provided feedback about this issue. Sidney would try to change but gave up quickly. Therefore, the people around Sidney gave up as well. This causes negative behavior on the part of others, especially passive aggressiveness and job turnover. So our advice is to listen to others and to learn from what they have to say.

On the basis of what you now know, please list your personal and professional strengths and areas that need development in the chart below.

My Strengths and Areas for Development

Personal areas of strength	*Personal* areas of development

Professional areas of strength	*Professional* areas of development

Once you're done, read over the list very carefully. Are you comfortable that you have captured everything that is important? Have you selected development areas that are meant to improve your career trajectory? Have you selected some personal areas of development to enhance your relationships or lifestyle? Is your thinking something that you would like to share with a key relationship to get additional feedback? If so, do it, and then let's move on.

What we fear doing most is usually what we most need to do.

—Ralph Waldo Emerson

It is our belief that individuals are always developing and never quite arrive at their fully developed stage. Individuals, throughout their lifetime, lose as well as gain strength, knowledge, and ability. If that is the case, then there is always something that a person can do to retain or enhance one's personal or professional skills or abilities. For example, Alex is trying mightily to lower his golf handicap—taking lessons, practicing, and setting goals. At work, he's focused on his writing and creative skills, hoping to hone them even further. Melissa is changing residences and lifestyles to accommodate a more active family life, while she also is making inroads to further build her business. What plans can you set for yourself that will enhance your personal and professional skills and abilities? Without any plan to work on these areas, there will be changes anyway, and like it or not, five years from now, your skill and ability levels will be somewhat different than they are today, even if you didn't work on them. Some new ones will be developed by serendipity, while others may erode and fall by the wayside. Having a disciplined plan to focus on these areas can create intentional change that will be positive for you.

We all have a tendency to depend on our natural strengths, sometimes overusing them to a point where they can become a negative—the strong orator who just talks too much, the individual performer who destroys the team.

Scott had impressive speaking ability. He could synthesize a number of different ideas and put them together in a way to make his audience understand the key aspects of the subject area. He did a lot of research and preparation for his talks. He was good at it. The problem was he was good at it for too long. He got to the point where his audience tuned out because Scott simply talked too much. He didn't know when to stop and didn't have sufficient breaks in his presentation. With a modest amount of change in his preparation and delivery, Scott's natural strength didn't have to turn into weakness.

JoAnne was an excellent writer. She did her homework and was able to write in a way that technical subjects could be easily understood by laypersons. She could make the point that she wanted to make but, unfortunately, would then go on to explain it in much more detail than was necessary. This, at times, confused the reader. It was just too much information. If JoAnne could learn to stop after making her point and not go on to explain it further, she could retain this creative writing strength.

Martin was on a sales call with his supervisor. After explaining the product to the potential buyer, Martin began to expound on the merits of the product. The client was impressed, agreed the product would meet her needs, and would certainly make the purchase. Martin went on to continue to describe and explain the product anyway. His supervisor interjected and said to the client that he was very glad that she appreciated their product and began to close the sale. After the meeting, the supervisor talked with Martin about the fact that he did a good job in the sales meeting but kept selling when he had already made the sale. In other words, he was strong enough to make the sale but had a weakness by not realizing when he had already made the sale and talking beyond what the client needed to make a decision.

These examples demonstrate how someone's strengths can devolve into weakness if they are not monitored. Looking at the chart you have filled out earlier in this chapter, choose an area where you need development and consider what step you might take to improve your performance.

Sometimes it is easy to do this, and sometimes it is trickier if you need a workaround for your situation. For example, there are courses one can take in finance, for the use of computer software, or for developing supervisory skills. Do you have a mentor or a coach? These individuals can help you to develop your emotional intelligence, your human resources acumen, or your planning skills. Whatever your level of financial or time commitment, whatever the skill level from which you start, there is always a way to find the path to self-development. If you need a no- or low-cost approach, you can use the public library for access to books or computers, or you can simply ask individuals who have the desired skill for individual training, perhaps in return for some work or skill you can provide for them instead of money. If you are short on time, there are things you can do that only take a few minutes a day, such as reading articles, viewing a webinar or online video, or speaking with a friend or business associate who has the skill you want to develop. Some organizations will support individuals who want to take courses or seek an advanced degree. Does yours? Using one's own funds to gain information and knowledge by buying books or magazine subscriptions, taking online courses, or going to conferences can also be a good investment. The important thing is to find the way that fits you and take it.

Lily decided to take a time-management course to improve her ability in this area. She also purchased a personal planner that she used to document how she was spending her time. This allowed her to see that some areas of time usage appeared to be disproportionate to what was required. She then took steps to reallocate her time and, by using the planner, could see the results.

Travis wanted to learn more about the industry in which he worked as a part of his career development. He began volunteering for training assignments that placed him in front of a group of people where he explained subject matter that he would first have to learn and then teach. He did this both inside his company and at industry conferences.

When Alex was a CEO, he would ask the vice presidents who reported to him what areas of development they would like to focus on. Each one then developed a plan for his or her development area. Alex would also select a few vice presidents and place them in charge of new areas of responsibility so that they could learn and perform under his tutelage until they were comfortable with the assignment. This was slightly risky for Alex, because he was ultimately responsible if they couldn't perform the task, but the payoff for the employees was huge, since they not only learned a new area of work but gained in confidence and competence as well. In addition, the organization now had a more fully developed individual with more knowledge to be applied to the organization's performance. Alex learned to do this as a part of his own development when several of his supervisors gave him similar opportunities.

We also believe that too many individuals focus so much on themselves and their work that they miss the keenly important developmental experience that comes from helping others. Volunteering your time or giving money allows you to help improve the lives of other human beings while at the same time learning things that don't come from a typical job.

Anne joined the board of the state chapter of her professional association. After spending a year on the education committee and learning what it meant to be a board member, she acquired some new skills and knowledge. One new lesson was how to develop and execute a major professional conference, something she had never done before. She also executed the contracts for the facility and speakers for the conference. The conference was so successful that Anne was elected as the board chair the following year. These new skills were transferrable to Anne's position at work and came earlier than she might have acquired them at her job. People who have broader engagement in their communities and a more expansive view of life are much more valuable to themselves and their organizations.

In our work at Rutgers University, we have programs that engage small groups of fifteen to twenty people for periods of up to two years focusing on their development and that of their organizations. We quite often see that individuals who are making progress on their personal development take on volunteer assignments as board members for nonprofits, or they raise money or help with projects. For example, Andrew had gained knowledge and experience that allowed him to develop a strategic plan for his business organization. He did this first by joining a nonprofit board and chairing a strategic planning committee of the board, which enabled him to transfer that skill back to his job. He ended up having the experience of developing the strategy of both a business and a nonprofit organization. He learned a great deal about the differences between these two types of organizations.

Are you working on any personal or professional development already? If so, document what it is and what your goals are for engaging in it. In addition to those areas you are already working on, choose at least two or three other areas in which you require personal or professional development. Decide what action steps you are willing to take as part of your plan to strengthen these areas or learn something new. How will you go about it? Whom will you talk to? What amount of time will you commit to it? Should you seek a mentor or a coach?

You've learned some things in thinking about your personal and professional self-development. Those lessons are important, so please note them in the box below.

What Have I Learned by Exploring My Areas of Personal and Professional Strength and Development?

_____

_____

_____

_____

_____

_____

_____

_____

Thinking about your learning and the examples provided earlier in this chapter, note in the chart on the following page the two or three areas in which you will take action. Please also include any areas that you are currently engaged in developing. Indicate some of the steps you will take and the time frame for completing your plans.

Consider the areas you want to develop first and the reasons why—are you seeking a promotion, do you want to close a knowledge gap, or is there an activity outside of work that you've always wanted to engage in? In other words, try to be intentional about the area you seek to develop by having a rationale for why you want to develop that area.

Actions for Areas That Need Development

Personal and professional development areas	Action steps to be taken	Time line for completion

You are essentially who you create yourself to be and all that occurs in your life is the result of your own making

—Stephen Richards, *Think Your Way to Success*

To initiate and sustain changes in yourself can take a day or a lifetime. The change that you seek can be made with grit and determination, but you have to mean it. And the only way to start is to start. Choose the area of development in which you seek change, commit yourself to that change, and take your first step. It will lead to the next.

Oliver was an attorney who wanted to learn more about the aerospace business. He had several clients in that industry and was beginning to develop an interest in the contributions that aerospace companies were making to the field of flight, especially space flight. He wanted to learn more, so he began reading extensively and took several courses at a local university. He decided to strike up more personal acquaintances with individuals in the field. His clients helped him to do this. He wanted to have a professional focus in this area and, as a result of his research and discussions, decided that his interest would be best served if he moved into a legal department of one of the companies. This was a life-changing decision for Oliver. His desire to have stronger knowledge and experience led to development, and that, in turn, led to an in-house counsel position with one of his previous clients.

Make the most of yourself . . . for that is all there is of you.

—Ralph Waldo Emerson

Individuals' strengths and their development activities can be deployed inside of organizations as well as individually. These organizations can be small or large businesses, government administrations, or nonprofit organizations. No matter the type of organization, they all have something in common; they each have a mission or purpose. They have organizational values, and each one has a distinct culture. In chapter 8, we will explore each of these areas, since they can have a profound impact on an individual's life and career.

CHAPTER 8

Organization Mission, Values, and Culture

Crossing Age Groups and Cultures

Personal Strengths and Development Areas

Work/Career

Current and Future Position

Organization Mission, Values, and Culture

Financial Plans

In this chapter, we define the mission, values, and culture of the organization in which you work or volunteer and compare it to what you have learned about yourself.

Just as you, an individual, have a personal mission or purpose and values, so too does the organization for which you work or volunteer. It doesn't matter if you are working for compensation or freely giving your time and effort in a volunteer activity; work is work. Whether it is a business, a government, or a nonprofit organization, a mission or purpose, values, and culture will exist within that organization. Aligning yourself with your organization, whether receiving compensation or not, is important for your own personal comfort and commitment.

Earlier in this book, you focused on writing your own mission or purpose statement, and you listed the personal values that are most important to you. At that time, you were able to see that purpose and values are the strong driving forces that move you ahead in life and shape your behavior.

The day-to-day behavior demonstrated by the leaders and others within an organization creates a culture in which everyone is operating. Most organizations have a mission statement; some will also publish their operating values, and a few will describe their desired culture.

Mission/Purpose

The purpose or mission statement is a "declaration of an organization's core purpose and focus that normally remains unchanged over time." It "serve[s] as a filter to separate what is important from what is not," to accept or reject ideas, products, and programs, to help focus on markets to be served, and to create an intended direction for everyone in the organization. A mission is the thing to be accomplished in order to achieve the organization's vision,[1] much the same as an individual's purpose drives one toward one's new future.

In Bill George's book *True North*, he says, "The most empowering condition of all is when the entire organization is aligned with its mission, and people's passions and purpose are in sync with each other."[2] Here are some mission statements from various types of organizations:

- Federal Aviation Administration (FAA): "Our continuing mission is to provide the safest, most efficient aerospace system in the world."

- Federal Department of Homeland Security: "With honor and integrity, we will safeguard the American people, our homeland, and our values."
- The American Red Cross: "The American Red Cross prevents and alleviates human suffering in the face of emergencies by mobilizing the power of volunteers and the generosity of donors."
- The Metropolitan Museum of Art: "The mission of The Metropolitan Museum of Art is to collect, preserve, study, exhibit, and stimulate appreciation for and advance knowledge of works of art that collectively represent the broadest spectrum of human achievement at the highest level of quality, all in the service of the public and in accordance with the highest professional standards."
- Google: "Google's mission is to organize the world's information and make it universally accessible and useful."
- Kellogg's: "Nourishing families so they can flourish and thrive."
- Ben & Jerry's has a three-part mission statement that guides its decision-making:

> Our Product Mission drives us to make fantastic ice cream—for its own sake.
> Our Economic Mission asks us to manage our Company for sustainable financial growth.
> Our Social Mission compels us to use our Company in innovative ways to make the world a better place.

As you can see, organization mission or purpose statements can be quite different. Some statements are developed solely by the leaders of an organization. Other statements can be the result of a planning process engaging most of the staff with one of the products of that process being a mission or purpose statement. The key is to be sure that individuals within the organization understand the mission or purpose of the company and that they have an individual commitment to that mission or purpose. To the extent that individuals don't buy into or don't have such a commitment, mission attainment is not going to be possible. That's one of the reasons we recommend as much engagement as possible with employees in an organization when developing the organization's mission statement. Organizations utilize training and education programs in order to mitigate employee disengagement, many containing examples of how the mission plays out in their environment, to promote the mission and to assure its acceptance.

According to Stephen R. Covey, "An organizational mission statement—one that truly reflects the deep shared vision and values of everyone within that organization—creates a great unity and tremendous commitment. It creates in people's hearts and minds a frame of reference, a set of criteria or guidelines, by which they will govern themselves."[3]

Values and Culture

Truly understanding an organization's values and culture can be difficult. This difficulty occurs when the stated values and culture do not line up with the behavior of the people in the organization. You may recall from your earlier work in this book that you have a set of personal values. Organizations do as well. They are standards that guide conduct. They might be thought of as a moral compass for an organization's business practices. Values and mission provide direction and focus to accomplish goals. Values express those things that individuals and organizations believe in. They can serve as decision-making tools and guide behavior.[4]

The myth of management is that your personal values are irrelevant or inappropriate at work.

—Stan Slap, *Bury My Heart at Conference Room B*

Nils, a client, was the CEO of a midsized company. He had a very talented and energetic executive staff. One of his vice presidents came to him with a product idea that was very exciting. The company was focused on building high-end residential housing. The product proposal suggested developing shopping centers near the high-end housing. Nils decided to bring the concept into one of the staff meetings with his executive group. After some in-depth discussion, it became evident to all that the company's mission of "providing high-end residences to individuals in the most attractive areas in our state and neighboring states," when used as a filter for decision-making about the product proposal, resulted in rejection of this new idea.

Nils could have taken a different course. He could have asked for some in-depth research on the shopping center idea that might have included information on companies that develop both shopping centers and residential housing. That in turn could have led to a change in the company's mission. However, the company's current mission was being deployed in a very successful way, which led to the conclusion to stay the course.

In the book *Built to Last*, Jim Collins and Jerry Porras note, "Core values equal the organization's essential and enduring tenets—a small set of general guiding principles; not to be confused with specific cultural or operating practices; not to be compromised for financial gain or short-term expediency." They go on to state, "Visionary companies tend to have only a few core values, usually between three and six."[5]

One famous case demonstrating values clash can be seen in the Wells Fargo Corporation, one of America's largest banks. Wells Fargo describes its five primary values this way:

- What's right for customers. We place customers at the center of everything we do. We want to exceed customer expectations. . . .
- People as a competitive advantage. We strive to attract, develop, motivate, and retain the best team members . . . to serve customers.
- Ethics. We're committed to the highest standards of integrity, transparency, and principled performance. . . .
- Diversity and inclusion. We value and promote diversity and inclusion in all aspects of business and at all levels. . . .
- Leadership. We want everyone to lead . . . in service to customers.[6]

It was shocking then to learn in September 2016 that the bank had fired fifty-three hundred workers over several years for creating millions of fake accounts primarily for the purposes of achieving personal and unit goals. This led to the company paying out a $185 million fine in civil penalties to atone for dishonest sales practices.[7] The company's CEO was replaced, and the staff was relieved of the unrealistic sales goals that had prompted the whole mess. The board was changed as well as its leadership. Wells Fargo's business and reputation has been hurt.

In addition to the predatory sales practices, customers were inappropriately charged mortgage fees and forced into buying unnecessary car insurance. The bank also set aside $285 million to refund foreign exchange and wealth-management clients. There was more fallout as well. Suffice it to say that the behavior of individuals inside the Wells Fargo organization did not reflect the company's stated values. It is now working hard to restore its business and its reputation, but one can only wonder what it might have been like to be an individual working in this culture and seeing the constant clash between the company's stated values and the behavior of its employees.

PepsiCo is the second-biggest food and beverage company in the world. Its CEO (through 2018) and current chairwoman is Indra K. Nooyi. She has consistently ranked on the *Forbes* list of the world's one hundred most powerful women. An organization's values and traditions and the way people work define its culture. Culture is reinforced by the tone that is set at the top of an organization.[8]

PepsiCo's stated values are,

- Care for our customers and the world we live in
- Sell only products we can be proud of
- Speak with truth and candor at all times
- Balance short-term and long-term
- Respect others and succeed together[9]

Over the past decade, the company has been dramatically transformed. It has expanded internationally and shifted its products into healthier beverage and snack choices. Nooyi steered this change in spite of opposition from investors. Today half of the company's revenues come from healthier beverage and snack products. Although Nooyi had to spend a good deal of time defending her strategy to critics, she was focused on the organization's values, especially care for the customer and selling products of which the company could be proud. At the same time, she was balancing short- and long-term risks and benefits. Hers is a case of values aligning with leadership behavior. Since she took over, company revenues have grown to $63.5 billion from $35 billion in 2006, while the company's share value has doubled.[10] Now imagine how an individual working in this company might feel about the experience, and contrast that to your reaction to the same question about a Wells Fargo employee.

PepsiCo is doing well, and Wells Fargo is attempting to restore its reputation. Organizational and individual reputation can be very quickly eroded, and restoring it can take a very long time. The guardrails against a company's eroding of reputation is having a strong mission and values statement and building a culture that rejects behaviors that are not compatible with those values.

Great leaders create great cultures regardless of the
dominant culture in the organization.

—Bob Anderson, *Mastering Leadership*

When Alex became CEO of American Field Service, he found himself and the organization in a turnaround situation. Among the organization's values was to be financially sustainable. However, for several years, the finances of the company were in a deficit position or just about breakeven. Alex decided to use this organizational value to focus the staff's attention on becoming financially viable. He announced that compensation increases and bonuses would only be paid if the end of the year saw profitability. He went on to seek staff input on as many good ideas as possible that could lead to this result. The organization became profitable in his first year as CEO. This is an example of how organizational leaders can create a focus within the organization on the basis of the company's stated mission or values that can lead to desired results.

Putting It All Together

Your organization's mission or purpose—its reason for existing and its goals for the future— should be discernable to you, even if it is not officially documented anywhere. Can you figure out to what purpose all the effort by the organization's people and resources is directed? How do you view your organization's purpose, even if your organization does have an official mission statement? Does your impression of what is really happening within the organization match what the company says it stands for?

The organization's values exist, whether officially accounted for or not, and are seen in the behavior of your coworkers and organizational leaders. If you like, go back to the listing of personal values we previously provided to see which values you hold that are also prevalent in your work culture. Is the culture comfortable for you, or are you repelled by it?

List your organization's mission and values on the following page. If the company has not published a mission statement or its values, then state what you believe them to be. Opposite these, please write your own personal mission statement (chapter 5) and values (chapter 3).

My and My Organization's Mission and Values

My organization's mission statement	My personal mission statement

My organization's values	My personal values

Can the values the organization says it has actually be seen in the behavior of the individuals within the organization? If these behaviors can be seen, then they are extant and true values. If the behaviors you observe in your coworkers are different from the stated values, then the stated values are not true. What do you think? Are your organization's values truly held by its employees? If not, what organizational values do your colleagues embody?

Some organizations might focus on teamwork as a value. But if staff members are highly competitive and don't share information or support one another on team projects, it's pretty easy to discern that lip service is being given to this value. In other organizations, a value might be the development of human resources. That organization might have a substantial number of training programs, provide for rotational assignments, and have a tuition-reimbursement policy. The values and company behavior alignment is more easily seen here. Think about this for your own situation and organization.

Just as your personal mission statement (chapter 5) describes why you are here and what your purpose in life is, the organization's mission statement should do the same for the organization. Does it? It is important that the organization's mission and values support your own mission and values (chapter 3). Do they complement each other? Does your organization allow you to deploy your personal mission within it? Do your personal values resonate within the organization, or do you have a conflict? Do your organization's formal and informal mission and values provide support to the life balance that you seek (chapter 6)? Do they enhance the relationships that you have, both personally and professionally (chapter 4)? Do they provide opportunities and room for you to develop personally and professionally (chapter 7)? Are you comfortable within the culture of your organization? If you can answer yes to these questions, then the organization's mission, values, and culture are compatible with those aspects of your life that are important to you and that will help you to achieve your life and career plan. Go back and look at the work you've done in the previous chapters in this book. If there is a major clash between your life goals and what the organization stands for, you will have to rethink what is attainable in your current work situation. You may even have to consider whether you should go elsewhere to gain the support that you require. On the other hand, if you have a pretty good match, then why not think about taking advantage of the culture that you're in?

I came to see, in my time at IBM, that culture isn't just one aspect of the game; it is the game. In the end, an organization is nothing more than the collective capacity of its people to create value.

—Louis Gerstner, chairman of the board and chief executive officer of IBM, 1993–2002

Are you comfortable with the culture of the place in which you work? The organizations that we work for create a day-to-day reality for us that flows in the direction we are headed or causes us to have to swim upstream. Either we enjoy working with the people we see every day, or we don't. The processes, programs, and policies of the organization energize us, or we are deflated. We accept or admire the organizational leadership team, or they embarrass us. We believe we are being treated fairly and are recognized for our contributions, or we are being taken advantage of and seem to be just a cog in the machine. Either we are driven toward the culture of the organization we work for, or we are repulsed by it.

If there is a match between you and your organization's mission, values, and culture, you are a lucky person and can focus on your life and career plan in a positive way. If there are clashes or conflicts that you see between the organization you work for and yourself, you can still have a positive life and career plan. However, there are two things you may have to ask yourself to be able to move ahead in a positive fashion. The first is whether you can fulfill your life and career goals working within your current organization. For example, would a change of leadership within your company or in your department or unit allow the diminution of the conflict you feel? What if you changed positions within the company? Second, if the organizational change that you seek is not possible, can you face the prospect of having to change organizations and jobs? Essentially, this means that you are so uncomfortable where you are that you don't see the possibility to achieve your life and career goals, are dealing with conflicts or clashes with the culture at work, and have to find a totally new environment to get what you want out of life.

In the book *Primal Leadership* by Daniel Goleman, Richard Boyatzis, and Annie McKee, it is noted, "When leaders operate with dissonant styles, the resulting culture is inevitably toxic." The authors provide an example from one company: "Despite the company having public service and education as its explicit mission, the president focused instead on short-term profit. . . . Also troubling was that he openly expressed how little he cared about employees' welfare. 'Bring 'em in and burn 'em out' he liked to say. . . . That leader's negative style underpinned a set of highly destructive cultural norms."[11]

As a young executive, Alex found himself in a department within a larger organization that didn't mirror the overall culture of the organization. In other words, the culture in the department was not a good fit, but the organization as a whole attracted him. Eventually a job change within the organization brought Alex into a new department, and that change made him much more comfortable and allowed him to progress in his career. He could not have stayed at that company without the change.

Josie told us about the time that she worked in a training department and was asked by her supervisor to sign off on a list of trainees indicating that they had attended a particular training course. Outside auditors were coming to the company to determine course attendance, and the paperwork had to be up-to-date. The trouble was that the individuals on that list had never attended the course that she was being asked to say that they had attended. Josie refused to sign off on the attendance sheet. She thought for sure her boss would fire her. That didn't happen. However, in less than a year, Josie left her position, because she recognized that her personal values clashed with the organization's culture.

Frank worked in a fairly large personal service firm and noted that the strength of the clientele base that he built was not recognized by his firm's leadership at the level he believed it should be. He thought that the culture of the company was built around taking for granted those individuals whose performance excelled. During our discussion, it became evident that he was quite interested in expanding his part of the business. He agreed to approach the firm's leadership with a plan to expand his area, coupled with a desire to see the firm better recognize its top performers. In other words, he had a plan to do both something for himself and something for the culture of the organization. He was successful in his attempt, stayed with the firm, and served in an important leadership capacity.

Olivia was feeling extreme pressure from one of the executives with whom she worked. The executive was a workaholic, and Olivia felt that she was turning into a workaholic herself. She wanted a much more balanced life as well as more interesting work. She applied for other positions in the organization but wasn't satisfied with the results. Eventually she decided that she had to leave the organization to get what she wanted. As her consultant, we helped her launch a job search that was supported by the mission, values, and culture match that she so very much desired.

These examples provide a small part of the picture that so many individuals have lived through in their work and career. Just as there is no perfect life, there is no perfect job. We are quite fortunate when we can get 80 percent of what we want in our workplace, and this, in turn, gives us the strength to handle the other 20 percent. If in your case you have a good match with your company on mission, values, and culture, see if you can get what you want where you are by tweaking one or two things to make it more comfortable for you. However, if you are in a state of conflict and you are uncomfortable in your workplace, then have the courage to make the move you need to make to achieve your life and career goals. Is there anyone you can talk to about your conflict inside your company? Are you ready to begin a job search? Are you comfortable where you are and want to enhance your position within the company?

Our number one priority is company culture. Our whole belief is that if you get the culture right, most of the other stuff like delivering great customer service or building a long-term enduring brand will just happen naturally on its own.

—Tony Hsieh, CEO of Zappos

What have you learned about the mission, values, and culture of the organization in which you work or volunteer? Document the key lessons in the box below.

What Have I Learned by Exploring the Mission, Values, and Culture of My Organization?

_____

_____

_____

_____

_____

_____

_____

Based on these lessons and the examples provided in this chapter, what actions should you consider for your life and career plan? Note them in the box below.

Ideas for My Action Plan

1. _____

2. _____

3. _____

4. _____

All of your good work up to this point is going to be beneficial in helping you achieve your life's goals. However, the one resource that we all require, whether we live modestly or extravagantly, is a strong financial base. Commensurate with your lifestyle, the amount of money you want or need will be a result of your life's purpose, values, and vision. In chapter 9, we want to help you create the financial foundation necessary for a healthy, attainable, and desirable future.

CHAPTER 9

Financial Plans

Crossing Age Groups
and Cultures

Personal Strengths and
Development Areas

Work/Career

Current and
Future Position

Organization Mission,
Values, and Culture

*Financial
Plans*

The purpose of this chapter is to focus on the extremely important need for individuals to develop a realistic financial plan regardless of current age or financial status.

A life without a financial plan is like a boat adrift in the sea. You just won't know if you can weather a storm or where your boat will land or if it will land at all unless you have a plan. If you do nothing else when reading this book, pay attention to this chapter and be sure to take action with what you learn. The contents of this chapter are one of the greatest gifts that we can give to a reader because all of your life plans should be based on a realistic view of your financial life. Your financial position will either support your plans or cause them to crumble.

Too many people shy away from thinking about their current and future financial status. Our day-to-day worries and financial concerns eat up our time and prevent most of us from thinking ahead more than the next several months or a year. In our practice and in our teaching, we have met many people who are financially ill prepared no matter what their career. When the individuals attending our seminars are asked if they have a financial plan, typically, only about 25 percent of them say that they do. After some questioning, it turns out that fewer than one in ten actually has a financial plan.

To find out if individuals have a financial plan, the first question we usually ask attendees is, When are you going to die? We know that you can't exactly predict when your death will happen. However, we all know that it will eventually happen. We have trouble thinking about it sometimes, but it will. To have a meaningful financial plan, one of the inputs required to create a financial time line is the approximate year that you believe you're going to die. Tough stuff! Nevertheless, there are ways to base your choice of a date on some facts:

- How long did your mother, grandmother, father, and grandfather live? At what age did they die? Were there any prevalent family illnesses moving among the generations?
- How is your health? Are you relatively healthy? Do you have health problems that can be life shortening? Or problems experienced by past or present family members?
- On average, what do the experts say about your life expectancy? Life insurance companies make their profits based on their best prediction as to when people will die. You can consult an actuarial

table from any life insurance company on the internet—enter your age and health, and get a response telling you, on average, how long you're expected to live. Just try searching for "life expectancy calculator" online.

Family history, personal health, and life expectancy are among the three most important factors needed to make a prediction for planning purposes about when you are going to die. Other factors include income level and even some hobbies. For example, when Alex first visited his financial planner with his wife, which they do now every two years to update their financial plan, the planner said that he wanted to be exceptionally conservative and therefore planned for Alex and his wife to live to age ninety-five. For Alex's wife, that seemed reasonable based on her responses to these same three questions just noted. Age ninety-five didn't seem realistic to Alex when he responded to the questions, and he wanted to plan to age ninety instead. Ultimately the planner convinced Alex to extend his plan to age ninety-five, because of the need to be sure of one thing—that Alex and his wife didn't run out of money before their deaths. This is why you need to predict when you believe you might die, because without that prediction, you won't know whether your income and assets are sufficient to support you for your lifetime. For a couple currently at age sixty-five, at least one of them will probably live to ninety years of age. Will he or she have sufficient financial assets at that time? Would you? According to an online calculator maintained by the Society of Actuaries (SOA), a sixty-five-year-old man has a fifty-fifty chance of living another seventeen years to age eighty-two. So for someone who retires at age sixty-five and stops earning work income at that time, the question is whether he or she will have enough money to last for the next seventeen years or more.

One thing you can do is to estimate your own general life expectancy using the cues we discussed earlier and consulting an online life expectancy calculator. On the following page is an example of how you might write it out, followed by space for you to write out your own family information.

If you start working at age twenty and retire at age sixty, there's a good chance you'll spend as many years in retirement as you did working.

—Michael Bivona, *Retiring? Beware!!*

My Life Expectancy

My family history:	My mother, grandmother, father, and grandfather lived a long life. Each of them passed away between the ages of eighty-eight and ninety-four. There were no prevalent family illnesses among the generations.
My health:	I am fifty-two years old and in good shape. I exercise, maintain a good weight, am educated, and have a good job.
What do the experts say with their life expectancy calculator?	Life expectancy is ninety-three [based on online assessment]
My conclusion:	As a result of my responses to these questions, I need to plan to have income to support me until at least age ninety-five.

Your turn:

My family history:	
My health:	
What do the experts say with their life expectancy calculator?	
My conclusion:	

The second question we ask our clients or attendees at our seminars is, When exactly will you retire and stop working? This is an important question, because when you stop working, your work income ceases. It is at that point that your money must come from sources other than work. Of course, you might choose to keep working part-time, and that income will then become part of your financial plan.

When you stop working, your sources of income might include personal investments, 401k or 403b plans, IRAs, savings, Social Security, income from rental properties, or perhaps pensions from your past employers. Knowing the date that your income stops or is greatly diminished is important, because you can fix the date of your death in your plan and you can fix the date your income will stop from work sources.

Predicting when you will die and when you expect work income to stop will give you the number of retirement years that you need to be supported by savings, investments, and other nonworking income like Social Security. Without the answers to these two questions and the question to follow, you won't have a good estimate for your financial plan as to whether you can support your lifestyle after you finish working.

So how does an individual decide when to stop working? The answer for each person can be quite different. To help you think about when you might want to retire, here are some questions to ponder and to which you can document your response. This is important whether you are twenty-five years of age or fifty-five years of age, because financial planning for retirement should start as soon as possible, regardless of age.

- Are you the type of person who loves work and wants to continue to work as long as possible, maybe even beyond age sixty-five?
- If so, do you see yourself in full-time or part-time employment?
- Rather than having a specific retirement date when all of your income stops, do you see yourself just reducing your work week over time and eventually retiring?
- Are you an individual who simply can't wait to retire, to go on to the things that are important to you and your life away from work? This

could mean a normal retirement date for you, say age sixty-five, or it might mean you want to establish a financial plan that allows you to retire earlier than that. Perhaps you're fortunate in that the type of work that you do can be converted into a consulting practice. This allows you to continue to work at a pace that places you in a semiretired status.

You or your financial planner could create alternate scenarios when completing your financial plan: you could use different potential dates of retirement and show their impact on your future financial needs so that you can more adequately prepare for the situation that ultimately makes the most sense. You can either pick a specific date when your work income will stop or decide that you want to have some level of income, the amount of which you will need to predict, in your semiretirement years. Your choices here will become inputs into your financial plan.

The third question we ask our clients or seminar participants has several parts: How much money do you spend a year to support your lifestyle? What do you spend it on? Will your annual expenditure need to be less, the same, or more, to provide you the kind of lifestyle you want when you retire?

Some financial advisers say that retired people need at least 80 percent of the income they had prior to retirement in order to sustain their lifestyle in retirement. So what is your current income and annual expense budget? A good financial plan can help you to understand whether you are set up to have the lifestyle you desire in retirement or whether you need to make changes to how you live now in order to save for later.

Individuals have different expectations for their time in retirement. Some want to spend more time traveling; others want to spend more time with family. Still others prefer to move to a warmer climate, perhaps to purchase a home. Still others want to take up long-desired hobbies like cycling, painting, or volunteering. You need to envision just what you would like your retirement to be and attach to it the lifestyle costs that will support your vision. The amount of money you need is a function of your needs and your desires. The ability to be able to produce that money now and into the future, so that you're ready for retirement, starts with a good financial plan and the actions required to build that supporting base.

To help you to think about this, complete the chart below. If you don't currently have a financial plan, you can estimate the amounts for each category. Now is the time to give yourself some idea of not only what finances support your current lifestyle but your expectations for your future lifestyle. You may be spending on education today but will not need to do so tomorrow. Your housing costs may be higher today because of the size of home or family that you have now, but you expect to downsize in the future. You may not spend very much on vacations now, but you may expect to do so when you retire. Your responses to these prompts will help you to build your financial plan so that it is realistic and reflects how you want to live.

Current and Projected Income and Expenses

Income	My current income	My expected retirement income
Salary	$	$
Rental income	$	$
Investment income	$	$
Social Security	$	$
Other	$	$
Other	$	$
Total	$	$

Expenses	My current expenses	My expected retirement expenses
Housing	$	$
Home maintenance	$	$
Food	$	$
Clothing	$	$
Insurance	$	$
Automobile	$	$
Vacations	$	$
Entertainment	$	$
Education	$	$
Savings	$	$
Other	$	$
Other	$	$
Total	$	$

If you don't take care of your money, your money won't take care of you.

—Mac Duke, The Strategist

Some people will retire as soon as they can, while a segment of the population never retires and will always have work income or part-time reduced income. Then again, there is also a small segment of the population that has substantial income, perhaps from investments or maybe from an inheritance or sale of a business or just good fortune in one's career. If you're fortunate enough to be in that group, your need for a financial plan decreases, but it is not eliminated. Even multimillionaires need to manage their money, have good asset allocation, and understand the best use of the assets they have. People with substantial financial resources hire financial planners and managers to make sure that those resources are deployed in the best possible manner so that their and their families' lifestyle can be continually supported into the future.

You need to do a financial plan to find out if you will have an adequate revenue stream to support your lifestyle after you stop working. In other words, when you do the analysis, you may find out that you can't stop working when you hoped to stop working.

In addition to the three questions to which you have responded earlier in this chapter, there are a number of aspects that make up financial plans that we will not fully comment on here but want to bring to your attention. They are issues that you must reconcile for yourself or discuss with a certified financial planner.

- **Taxes:** Taxes erode income over time. Federal, state, and local taxes are paid out of income and therefore reduce current income and the amount available for savings and spending. A good financial planner will advise you as to which of your assets or investments should be used first to obtain the best tax efficiency. Your plan will also estimate your future taxes.
- **Inflation:** All financial plans must have an annual inflation assumption. For example, Alex's financial plan has a 3 percent inflation assumption. This means that his plan assumes that each dollar of his savings will purchase 3 percent less every subsequent year. Inflation takes a bite out of savings and investments over time while increasing expenses.
- **An assumption regarding asset growth or decline:** Here you or a planner will probably use a conservative estimate of how much your assets

will increase annually due to growth, while they decline annually due to assets being used as income. For example, if you believe your after-tax income from assets is 5 percent and you intend to use 2 percent of your assets every year, when you couple that with a 3 percent inflation rate, your assets will be status quo.

- **Scenario planning:** A financial planner can provide various planning scenarios that tell you the chance of obtaining your goals under each of the scenarios. In other words, factoring in savings, expenses, earnings, and the like, a planner should be able to tell you that there is an 80 or 90 or 100 percent chance your plan will work and that you will not outlive your income from savings, investments, or other sources.

- **Lifestyle choices:** There are many choices one makes in the course of a life, some of which hugely impact your ability to save money, including your desire to purchase a first or second home, save for and pay for a child's education, or travel extensively. For example, Alex and his wife decided that when their first grandchild was born, they would invite their children, spouses, and grandchildren every other year to join them on a family vacation. This has been a very rewarding experience for all and gives the family a way to come together and share on a periodic basis. This is included in their financial plan.

One more thing needed by everyone who has a financial plan is insurance. Different types of insurance meet a variety of financial needs. For example, you might have life insurance in your financial plan so that in the event of your death you can help your family to have sufficient resources. This is especially necessary if you have not been able to save and invest enough money on your own to accomplish your financial goals.

Life insurance is meant to replace assets or income lost in the event of death. For example, Cole purchased term life insurance for the same number of years as his mortgage, thirty years. Should Cole die fifteen years from now, the term life insurance would provide enough money to pay off the remainder of his mortgage so that his family could stay in their home. Your planner should be able to discuss other types of insurance as well.

Louis was a client whose financial plan included the provision that one spouse would work and invest a set amount of income over a ten-year period. When we asked Louis what would happen if his spouse died, we were told that they had a sufficient amount of life insurance to make up for any loss of income over the ten-year period. Then we asked what would happen if the spouse became disabled and could not work? Louis was stunned. This couple had not thought about what would happen if the spouse who planned to work for ten years became disabled. You see, for younger and middle-aged individuals, it is more likely that your plans could be scuttled by disability than by death. It is not uncommon for disability to occur as a result of some trauma such as a fall, an automobile accident, or a sports injury. People who become disabled may lose their cognitive skills or the ability to walk or speak, and therefore to work, either temporarily or permanently. Therefore, disability insurance is a good investment as well, to guard against loss of income and savings in the event of disability.

A good financial planner can also advise you on personal liability or business interruption insurance or other forms of asset protection. The key is to make sure that included in your financial plan are those forms of insurance that if utilized can be integrated into your plan without creating challenges for you or your loved ones.

At this point, if you are actively and uncomfortably thinking about whether you have really made yourself ready for the future, join the club. Most people become uneasy thinking about their financial futures and whether they can really afford what they say they want, because it is often such a struggle to make ends meet in the day-to-day rush of our lives. But relax; there is a way forward.

**Every financial worry you want to banish and financial dream
you want to achieve comes from taking tiny steps today
that put you on a path toward your goals.**

—Suze Orman

First, let's review some of the actions you might take to develop a financial plan for yourself and your family. If you have a spouse or significant partner, we strongly suggest that he or she be involved in this with you. Howard, our client and the CEO of an organization, was frustrated because he could not get his wife to join him in a financial planning effort. We explained why it was important that they both understand the plan and what it would do for their life going forward and were surprised to learn that the major reason that his wife didn't want to engage in the planning was because she felt that the planner would surely recommend that they sell their luxurious home at some point in order to downsize and use the assets from the sale. She simply didn't want to hear this so refused to engage at all. Financial planning, at times, can involve a great deal of emotion. As a result, Howard never completed a financial plan during that time. That meant that the two of them were living in the present with a totally unknown future. Eventually, with encouragement, he developed a financial plan on his own and discussed it with his spouse. The key scenario in his plan did call for the sale of their home since the sale proceeds provided substantial retirement assets that were required to support his chosen lifestyle.

Financial planning helps you to discuss with those you love important issues about retirement, savings, where to live, planning for children, the details of your respective wills or estate plans, and so on. So, if you are alone, get moving on this task. If you have someone significant in your life, engage him or her in the planning at the outset. It works even better if that significant individual is one of your key relationships and has provided input to your overall life and career plan.

We have found in our teaching and consulting that our message about financial planning is not taken as seriously as it should be by younger individuals in the twenty- to thirty-five-year-old range. These young people, with exceptions, see the need for financial planning as something way off in the distance. After all, "Why talk about retirement when I'm twenty-seven years old?" The reason that this attitude concerns us is that the possibility of achieving one's long-term financial goals is greatly increased the earlier an individual thinks about it, acts on it, and makes decisions about savings and investments. Career decisions can be informed by an early financial plan. Decisions about marriage, having children, where to live, and so on can all be informed by having a financial plan. Having a financial plan at a young age can demonstrate the choices and options faced by the young person and how one choice or one option might be better than another for the person's long-term financial health. So if you're a young person reading this book and you think that planning for retirement is something that can wait, rest assured, it can't. Something as simple as committing to using only 30 percent of all compensation increases for lifestyle while 70 percent of the increase is saved or invested can have very meaningful impact on achieving financial goals.

There are a number of potential resources available to you to get started on your financial plan. You can pay for a financial planning service. Both large companies and individual financial planners provide these services. There are primarily two types of planners. "Fee-based" planners work with you and charge you by the hour or with a set fee to produce your financial plan. They do not usually help you to activate the plan, nor do they accept the management of any of your investments. Many people believe that this type of service is the most objective, because the only goal of this type of planner is to complete your plan. You know how much you will pay up front, and you know what you're going to receive in return. But because this is such an important task, I strongly suggest that you interview more than one fee-based planner.

There are also investment organizations that provide financial planning services to customers along with managing the implementation of your plan. They will manage all or some of your assets for a fee and will direct the investment of those assets, guided by the results of your completed financial plan. These organizations may be stockbrokers, life insurance companies, or money managers. As a matter of fact, there are some investment organizations that specialize in helping individuals in a specific market and will provide a plan to those customers at no charge if the company handles their investments as well. For example, TIAA-CREF's primary market includes individuals who are employed in educational or nonprofit organizations, while USAA focuses on members of the military. These companies don't provide a fee-only option; but these are larger companies, and you will usually get a good-quality product.

There should be good chemistry between you and the financial planner you choose, since financial plans are supposed to be updated every two to three years and you will want a strong relationship on which to depend. A good planner will be honest with you, always saying what you need to hear even if that makes you uncomfortable. A good planner plans with your interest at heart, not his or her own interest. The current range of fees charged by a fee-based planner is approximately from $1,500 to $5,000. The quality of what you receive depends on the experience of the planner and your active engagement with the planner.

No matter what resource you use, a good plan should include a main financial scenario noting year by year your expected financial status up to the time of your death. It includes such things as a realistic savings rate, inflation rate, and expected percentage of taxes. It will consider all of your assets, property, and insurance. The plan will tell you what your current net worth is and what your expected future net worth will be. Your annual expenditures in the plan will reflect your lifestyle and, as appropriate, include such things as children's education, expensive vacations, additional property investments aside from your home, and so on. Divorced or remarried individuals could require more focused advice in their situation. In addition, a planner should discuss with you the need you may have for a will, an estate-planning attorney, or a living will.

Please recognize that some plans can be very streamlined since the individual may not have a lot of complexity in his or her financial life. On the other hand, someone who owns a varied degree of assets including rental or other properties or exotic investment forms would require much more experienced and technical advice from a planner. Therefore, the planner that you use should match your financial reality.

The following websites are good resources where you may find examples of the contents of a financial plan. We do not endorse any of these sites in particular, but we do think that seeing examples of what to consider is helpful when evaluating your own financial plan:

- The College Investor: https://thecollegeinvestor.com/16990/ 6-elements-of-a-solid-personal-financial-plan/
- Hyre Personal Wealth Advisors: http://www.hpwealth.com/p/ essential-components-to-a-financial-plan
- Mercer Advisors: https://www.merceradvisors.com/blog/2014/03/ 19/8-key-components-of-financial-planning/

If you choose to use a financial planner, be sure that he or she is a certified financial planner (CFP). This means that the individual has passed the requirements of the CFP Board. You can find a financial planner by asking friends if they have one, going online for planners in your area, or contacting the CFP Board at https://www.cfp.net/ home. You can also ask your life insurance agent, your broker, or your bank, if you have them. Sometimes for individuals investing at work in 401k or 403b plans, the company handling those plans might provide financial planning as an added service at low or no cost.

If the cost of a financial planner exceeds your current budget, you can still get started. There are several websites that provide instructions on how to develop your own financial plan. Here are a couple of websites that you may refer to:

- SpreadsheetSolving: https://spreadsheetsolving.com/personal -finance-modeling/
- The Balance: https://www.thebalance.com/begin-saving-for -retirement-4073863

Each of these sites describes what's needed to develop your own plan. There will be a number of inputs that you will have to provide, such as current level of savings, current income, expected future income, the answers to the three questions that we asked earlier (longevity, expected retirement date, future lifestyle budget), and so on. Admittedly, the easier approach would be to find a financial planner at the lowest cost possible that fits your budget, but it is possible to come up with your own financial plan.

Financial peace isn't the acquisition of stuff. It's learning to live on less than you make, so you can give money back (to your fellow man) and have money to invest. You can't win until you do this.

—Dave Ramsey, author of financial books and radio host

The combination of a well-developed life and career plan coupled with a good financial plan is all you need to tell you where you are going and when or whether you can expect to arrive. In addition, the financial plan answers a number of key questions, for example,

- How much money do I need to save?
- At what time can I really afford to retire?
- Do I need to work part-time for income, or can I explore my passions?
- And, for some of us, if I die before my spouse, can my spouse afford to live the way we both hope he or she can live?

If you are young and start saving at the rate that you should, it will be so much easier for you to attain your life goals. The later you start to save and invest at the rate you should, the more difficult it will be for you to attain those goals. However, it is never, ever too late to start. The principle of compound interest comes into play. Compound interest is the addition of interest to the principal sum of a loan or deposit or, in other words, interest on interest. It is the result of re-investing interest, or positive returns, rather than paying them out, so that the earnings or interest in the next period are then earned on the principal sum plus previously accumulated earnings or interest. This means that your money will continue to grow over time if left untouched. For example, if your invested assets were earning 10 percent per year over seven years, those assets would double. This is why we strongly encourage individuals not to touch savings, especially the money saved in 401k, 403b, and IRA plans. These funds should only be used in extreme emergencies since they are meant to support you at a future time when work income ceases.

Although your life and career plan and your financial plan provide substantial information and a track to run on, they are also both decision-making tools. As we discussed earlier, the life and career plan should be used to help you make decisions about your life, such as leaving a job, accepting a new job, relationships that should be discarded or held tight, and so forth. A good financial plan might help you to answer such questions as these:

- Can I buy that second home?
- Does this new job offer provide enough income to meet my savings need?
- Can I afford the college my daughter wants to go to?

These two powerful tools, your life and career plan including your financial plan, can focus your thinking on these types of life-altering decisions and help you to make better choices. You can make a decision about your life and then plug the financial results of that decision into your financial plan and see if the plan meets your desired financial goals. If they are in conflict, then you have the time to adjust one or both of them until they are in alignment.

Constance and Mark wanted to purchase a second home for family vacations and weekend use. The cost of the second home was $400,000. They had enough money in savings and investments to purchase the home. However, they needed to understand the impact on their financial goals of using the $400,000 to purchase the home, since that money would no longer be available for gaining investment returns into the future. So they asked their financial planner to run a separate scenario in which the $400,000 was taken from their investments in order to purchase the home to see if he could tell them whether they could still reach the lifestyle income they desired in retirement. Their planner ran the numbers and told them that if they took $400,000 out of their savings to purchase the home, it would still provide a 90 percent chance of obtaining their financial plan goals. Constance and Mark thought that this small risk was worth it, and they went ahead with the purchase.

So, if you have both a life and career plan and your financial plan, you now have a motor on your boat, and you can take that boat, which is your life, where you want, bringing your significant others along with you. If you don't have a financial plan, don't procrastinate in getting one. It can take a lot of time, as much as four to six months, to put your plan in place. So do it now!

Your financial plan supports all aspects of the Life & Career Planning Model. Your work, your family, your interests, your development, all of it, will be enhanced if you have a solid financial plan to support you and your future.

—Alex J. Plinio

What have you learned about financial plans? Document the key lessons in the box below.

What Have I Learned by Exploring Financial Plans?

_____

_____

_____

_____

_____

_____

_____

_____

_____

_____

Based on these lessons and the examples provided in this chapter, what actions should you consider for your life and career plan? Note them in the box below. Certainly if you have a financial plan, you should be updating it at least every two years. And if you don't have a financial plan, your primary action should be to get one.

Ideas for My Action Plan

1. _____

2. _____

3. _____

4. _____

The results of your completed financial plan will greatly inform your review of your current career position and what a future position might entail. And that discussion will have a more nuanced and good-quality outcome if you know the results of your financial plan. Get your plan done as soon as possible, and, for now, let's begin an examination of your current and future career positions.

CHAPTER 10

Current and Future Position

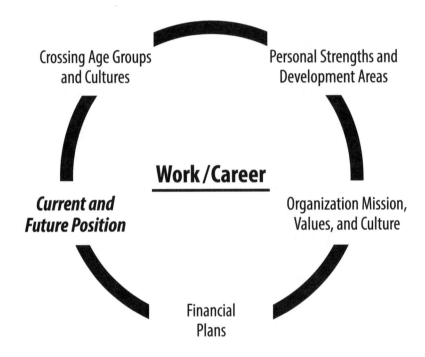

The purpose of this chapter is to compare your current position at work with each of the areas we examined about yourself earlier in the book. In addition, we need to uncover just what your next, future position will look like.

Mel was happy with her current job and employer. However, she did begin to wonder about her career in the long term. She wasn't quite sure as a forty-year-old woman with two children and a demanding job where she might want to steer her career over the next ten or twenty years. She began to ruminate about different career paths she might take and even thought about changing careers. She wasn't quite sure what to do. When she came to us, she was not unhappy with her current position at work, but she was unhappy with not knowing what her future might look like. Over time, Mel was able to explore options with us that eventually led her to make two key decisions. First, she decided she would not stop working and would continue to meld home, family, and work. Second, she had a desire to work at a higher executive level but decided that if she got the right job, it could be either with her current company or in a different company. That allowed Mel to plan a course of action that could invent her new future.

Nobody can go back and start a new beginning, but anyone can start today and make a new ending.

—Maria Robinson, author and expert on child development

Now let's take a look at your current position and where you are in your career. We need to compare what you said earlier in the model about yourself and what you were looking for in your job with your current position. Here are some key questions to consider; as you have been doing, please document your responses:

- Does the work that you do give you the opportunity for a positive work-life balance?
- Are you able to spend time outside of work on those things that are important to you? If not, why not?

- Are there any aspects of your work that are complementary to your interests, noted earlier?
- Are those interests found in your job, or does your current employer support them in an adequate manner outside of the work that you do?
- When you wrote about the things that provide you joy, are any of those things found in your current work and career?
- How do you rate the quality of your work relationships? Are any of them toxic? Or are they compatible and supportive?
- Does your organization and your current role allow for time needed to retain and build your relationships outside of work?
- Do your organization's values adequately match or clash with your personal values?
- Does the work you do in your current position support your personal values?
- Does your current position help you to attain your life's purpose or mission?
- Do you feel that this position puts you on the road leading to the attainment of your personal vision (chapter 12)?
- Does your current position provide you with sufficient skill, ability, and personal development?
- Is the current compensation you receive at work substantial enough to support your financial plan?

If you see compatibility in all or most of these areas, you probably enjoy your work and your employer and are happy to be doing what you are doing. However, if there are some very real discontinuities between your work and career and these areas of your self-examination, then you need to take action to resolve any tensions between your work and your personal life. These actions need to be a part of your life and career plan.

For example, if you have toxic relationships at work, how will you handle them? If work requires so many hours of your time that you have no time left over for family, friends, or your interests, what actions can you take to balance things? If you have a clash of values with your employer, is it resolvable? If your responses to these questions high-light specific areas that need improvement, you should try to resolve them at your current workplace before you decide to just leave your organization. You have an investment in your current job, and you should find out if you can get what you want from the organization before you sever the relationship.

If you need help, ask for it. Help can come from one of your key relationships or a mentor or from consultants or from books such as this one. Don't be concerned about asking for the help you need to work through any existing challenges that you have. Have a look at the resource listing in the "Resources" section of this book for places to begin. The main thing to remember is not to place yourself in a position where those things that are concerning you in your job begin to fester to the point that you believe they are not resolvable. It would be better to develop a plan to attack each issue as it impacts you rather than just to let the problem grow. Of course, there may be some risk in doing this, if your employer isn't open to hearing criticism or not flexible enough to accommodate any changes. How-ever, if you don't assume the risk, your challenges will probably not resolve themselves.

Cedric was a very experienced and knowledgeable technology executive. He had been working for his company's CEO for just over a year. When he came to us, he was upset, since the CEO, who was experienced in technology but not as much as Cedric was, contin-ually pushed back on Cedric when Cedric was taking independent action. The CEO wanted to control a broad array of decision-making as applied in the technology arena. He seemed to do it because he liked the field, rather than because it was necessary to get the desired results. Cedric liked the company and his position in it except for the fact that he and the CEO clashed more often than not over Cedric's independent role and the decisions he was making. Cedric was lucky. When we helped him to frame how he might approach the CEO to resolve this challenge, he met with success. The CEO just hadn't real-ized how much Cedric viewed his interaction as a hindrance. The CEO thought he was helping when in fact he was not. He and Cedric agreed that Cedric would be the one held accountable for the results of his actions and that the CEO would back off.

Expect to succeed even before you start. All winners, no matter what their game, start with the expectations that they are going to succeed. Winners say, "I want to do this and I can do this," not "I would like to do this, but I don't think I can."

—Denis Waitley, *The Psychology of Winning*

Another key question concerning your current position arises when you complete your financial plan. It is important to have a financial plan before you fully complete your life and career plan, as we discussed in chapter 9. Does your present work situation provide an income that supports the savings required for your financial plan? If it does, that's great. If it doesn't, do you see the possibility of increased compensation coming from your current employer? Or do you perhaps need to consider a reduction in your expenses? Or do you think you will need to change jobs to attain your goal? Considering this situation might prompt you to include actions in your life and career plan to resolve this issue.

Does your current job make use of your strengths while also providing opportunities for the professional development that you need? Here, too, asking for what you need from your current employer is really important. If you want to work more in a team environment, ask for it. If you need to learn more about finance or human resources, ask for that opportunity. If you would like a rotational assignment to another area, ask for it. If you work in a small business, perhaps the owner would consider giving you some time off to take a course or for you to attend an industry-related conference. Also, in a small business, you might ask to wear several hats for a specific period of time so you can learn new responsibilities. In other words, through what you've already identified as important to you from your life and career plan, take charge of your own development by having specific actions identified in your plan.

Be brave and take risks. You need to have faith in yourself. Be brave and take risks. You don't have to have it all figured out to move forward.

—Roy T. Bennett, *The Light in the Heart*

A key part of your life and career plan is the creation of a personal vision (chapter 12). When you create this later, we will remind you to go back and ask yourself, "Does my current work position place me on the correct path to achieve the ultimate vision that I have developed for myself?" If it doesn't, there must be additional action steps in your life and career plan to move you toward the path that is more likely to help you reach your vision.

Go back and systematically examine your responses to the prompts in the previous chapters, and compare your answers to your current position at work and the career trajectory you desire. Wherever incompatibilities arise, your life and career plan should target action steps to overcome the challenges presented by those incompatibilities. Each reader will have his or her own needs and set of actions. The important thing is not to bury the concerns that you identify but instead to highlight them, seek advice and assistance where needed, act on those concerns, and attempt to create a more compatible situation for the attainment of your life and career goals.

For example, when Sharon, a customer service supervisor, was developing her life and career plan, she contrasted her values with those of the organization leader for whom she worked and came away with some sobering findings. Although she was learning in her role, it came at a very high personal cost. Her manager often treated her harshly, sometimes in public. It was as embarrassing for her to know that her colleagues were forced to listen to her being dressed down as it was for her to endure the yelling and mistreatment. She had put up with this for almost a year and had come to us wanting to reevaluate her life. After completing her life and career plan, she tried to resolve the issue directly at work, unsuccessfully, and ultimately realized that she was better off in a new job, so she left.

You may be fortunate in finding that you have a good match between the things that you need in your work and career and your current role and employment. If that's the case, you're seeking to maintain your environment while finding opportunity to grow and advance. You also want to assure that your life outside of work is enjoyable because your current position allows for that. If, on the other hand, most of your needs are being met but there are a few areas requiring attention, those areas might fall into work relationships, professional development, or culture clashes. You may see these things as resolvable, and you will plan to take the steps necessary to get that resolution. A person in a more difficult situation is one who finds too many impediments at work to be able to have the career and life that he or she wants. He or she may consider these impediments irresolvable, and this in turn can lead to a search for a different position either inside or outside the current employer. Where are you on this continuum?

What Have You Learned about Comparing Aspects of Yourself with Your Current Organization and Role? Is There Any Potential Action That You Need to Consider?

_____

_____

_____

_____

_____

_____

I can do more than I think I am capable of. More than my experience base, education, background would let me think is possible.

—Scott Kelly, astronaut

_____

Now let's take a look at your next, future position. If you know where you are in your current position and you know where you would like your career to go, what is your next move? What is your next position? You might be a young person with a number of possible positions in front of you. You may be a midcareer person who needs to recognize that there may be only one or two next jobs in your career. Or you could be close to retirement and wondering about full retirement or part-time work or consulting. In any case, think about the appropriate next position that lines up with your mission, values, and career trajectory. What is it? Can you describe it? Write a job description for the position you envision, noting the key ingredients of the work you want to do as a part of your long career. Here is an example of a next-job description written by one of our clients, Mario, who wanted to take charge of his career. He was well liked and thought highly of by executives in his company, but he wanted a meaningful career and also wanted to make sure that he provided a desired lifestyle for his family.

My Next Job: Aligning with My Mission, Values, and Career Trajectory

I have been in my current middle-management position for three years. After assignments in administration and marketing, I was promoted and given the responsibility for the company's compensation and benefits programs. My performance has proven that I am in the top 20 percent of individuals having my type of role and responsibility. I would like to stay with my company. My next position would be one in which I would manage managers as a first-line executive. My career has spanned administration, marketing, and human resources. Of these three areas, I would like my next position to be in human resources. I would hope to have managers reporting to me who are responsible for employee recruitment, training, talent management, and benefits. In this role, I would like to report to the head of human resources for my company.

The upward movement I am describing would increase my compensation and my visibility in the company. It aligns with my career trajectory, which calls for me to be a business division head within the next five years. I believe that my background in administration, marketing, and human resources creates a positive alignment for me to achieve this goal within my organization.

This next position would align with my personal values and would enable me to influence the organization's values. I could help to set tone at the top. I also believe that I can both perform in this role and have an appropriate life balance for myself and my family, which can also serve as a signal to my staff and employees about the kind of work valued by the company.

We have advised individuals who see themselves as professionals in a specific career. They want to stay in that role, not change jobs but advance in the profession. Others who have come to us like their industry and the type of work that they do and see opportunity outside their current organization. Still others value diverse experiences. They want to move into different positions in their organization or perhaps even outside their sector, for example, from business to nonprofit or vice versa. For you, one key to the door of your future is to be intentional about how you want to manage your career and where you ultimately want it to go. There is nothing wrong with staying in place in a profession, nor is there anything wrong with deciding to move to different positions or different sectors. What would be wrong for you is that you haven't even thought about it.

Now it's your turn. What's your next job? What skills do you want to develop? How does the future job align with your mission, values, and career trajectory? Refer to the example above, be as specific as possible, and include such things as compensation, geographic location, and alignment with your self-evaluation including life balance.

My Next Job: Aligning with My Mission, Values, and Career Trajectory

_____

_____

_____

_____

_____

_____

_____

_____

_____

_____

_____

_____

_____

_____

Now you have examined where you are in your current role in your organization, and you have an understanding of what you would like your next move to be. When you create your life and career plan, it will include the action steps necessary to begin to move toward your next position. You will have to answer a number of questions for yourself to create those actions, for example,

- If I work in a small company, is it the owner that I have to talk to?
- If I work in a larger organization, is it best to start with my own boss or perhaps someone in human resources?
- How do I prepare to tell my story to whomever I'm going to talk to?
- Do I have a mentor who can help me?
- Is the timing of my request now, or should I wait?
- How will I sell myself without being too aggressive but still let important people know what I have planned for my career and my life and that I need their help to attain my vision?

Set specific goals in your plan:

- Who am I going to talk to and when?
- What is the time line for getting this done?

- What materials or information do I need to have before I start my discussions?
- Do I know anyone at the executive level who can give me advice in a confidential manner?
- How long am I willing to wait to achieve this goal?

Each of your actions should lead to goals that are specific, measurable, attainable, realistic, and timed.

Here is an example of a situation that you might face in your current job, as well as an action and goal: Sean told us that he moved into a new position at work. He expected to perform in this role for twelve to eighteen months before moving on to his desired next position. Unfortunately, one of his coworkers seemed to see Sean as a threat to his own position in the company. Since Sean and his coworker performed similar functions on the sales support team, they interacted on a fairly frequent basis. Sean was uncomfortable and knew that he had to do something to repair the relationship if he were to stay on target to his next job. Sean knew that if the situation was left unattended, it could impede his career progress. After our counseling, he decided that his goal was either to improve that relationship or to avoid as many interactions as possible with his coworker. Sean outlined the following steps to try and resolve the problem:

1 I will talk with this person, explaining my concerns in a nonconfrontational manner to determine if improvement in the relationship is possible.

2 I will have this meeting no later than _____ (specific date).

3 On the basis of the results of the meeting, I will work toward the improved relationship or find ways to work around this particular individual.

4 Should the relationship impede my career progress, I will seek advice from either my manager or the human resources department.

5 If this relationship continues to hinder me in my progress, I will have to move to a different position. I should do this no later than six months from the date of the meeting with my coworker.

In another case, Gary was quite comfortable in his position. He knew that he needed a rotational assignment. He understood where his next role in his current company should be but had to move to a different department to get the experience he desired. He didn't have a challenge like Sean's to overcome. He could move directly to create a plan that would have the potential to get him to the next job.

Here is an example, similar to Gary's, of a goal and specific actions related to finding your next position:

1   I will share the next job position description I created with a key relationship, mentor, or manager whom I respect.

2   By _____ (date), I will discuss with my immediate supervisor his or her views of my next position and obtain an opinion on the position and its attainability by _____ (date).

3   I will approach the human resources department to determine if my goals are realistic, and I will do this by _____ (date).

4   I will determine if additional training or education can help me attain my next position. I will do this by _____ (date).

5   If I find that I cannot obtain my desired next position in my current organization, I will begin a job search by _____ (date).

At this juncture, you could be on a path to maximize your current position or to move toward your future position. It is not possible in this book to provide examples of actions for all kinds of different career fields. For instance, what if you want to go into your own business? Such things as obtaining business investments, assessing life balance, and the risk of failure would loom large. Or how would you handle these actions in a personal service firm like a law firm or a CPA firm? Here, such things as your area of expertise and your relationship with your partners would have major impact. What if you work in a smaller nonprofit organization? And so on. This book can't cover all the bases, but it can provide a way of thinking that can be applied in various settings where individuals might find themselves.

When one door closes, another opens, but we often look so long
and so regretfully upon the closed door that we do not see the
one that has opened for us.

—Alexander Graham Bell

What Have You Learned by Thinking about
Your Current and Future Position?

_____

_____

_____

_____

_____

_____

_____

_____

_____

_____

_____

Document Here, for Consideration Later, Potential Actions That Come to Mind or Considerations for When You Do Your Action Plan

Current Position	Future Position
1. _____	_____
2. _____	_____
3. _____	_____
4. _____	_____
5. _____	_____
6. _____	_____

Life is a moving, breathing thing. We have to be willing to
constantly evolve. Perfection is constant transformation.

—Nia Peeples, singer and actress

Today we are all faced with having to recognize and engage with various cultural and age groups in the workplace. The diversity of cultures within the United States and around the world is both broad and complex. In addition, individuals belong to one of five different and distinct age groups found in today's workforce. With a better handle on understanding differences in culture, diversity, and age groups, you will be better prepared when activating your life and career plan.

CHAPTER 11

Crossing Age Groups and Cultures

The purpose of this chapter is to explore the fact that individuals in different age groups and from different cultures can be better communicated with if you know something about these age groups and cultures before deploying your life and career plan.

In your life and career, you will come into contact with many individuals who may not view life in the same way you do. Later, as you activate your life and career plan, it is important to recognize that you are a part of many different cultures. You have a family culture, a business or organization culture, a state or national culture, or maybe even a subgroup culture, like a club you belong to or a subset of human beings. In addition, you, as does everyone, belong to a specific age group that has distinct characteristics—many, but not all, of which you may embody yourself. It is helpful when deploying your life and career plan to understand the generational differences among groups of people and also to gain a better understanding of intercultural competence.

Generational Differences

Susan was sixty-two years old and contemplating whether to open her own business or stay with her current company. To better understand her options within the company, she had to talk to two people: her manager, who was forty-two years old, and her human resources representative, who was thirty-three years old. Susan was a Baby Boomer about to talk to a Generation Xer and a Millennial. Did it matter how she communicated with each of these individuals? Would different forms of communication, one for each, help her? What phrasing would be more appealing to each of these individuals? How might she achieve her goals through better communication? As we move through this chapter, you will be able to determine what could benefit Susan, and you will be in a better position to understand how you also might communicate with people in your own life who are from different backgrounds or age groups.

In the workforce in the United States today, as well as in other developed countries around the world, there are five specific age groups. These age groups are born roughly in the following time frames:

- Traditionalists: 1928–1945
- Baby Boomers: 1946–1964
- Generation X: 1965–1980

- Millennials: 1981–1998
- Generation Z: 1999 to present[1]

There are significant differences in how these five age groups perceive themselves, and there are specific differences in how they would like to be treated in communication, supervision, and the working environment. As you set your life and career plan in motion, the individuals whom you talk to and those from whom you will seek help could be in any one of these age groups. Having some insight about them in a general sense could be helpful.

For example, the Traditionalists like communication that is one-on-one or written in a formal, logical manner. Baby Boomers prefer communication delivered in person whenever possible and spoken in an open and direct style. Generation Xers prefer that you get straight to the point and use facts, and they value email as a preferred method of communication. Millennials prefer to communicate in their networks and teams using multimedia while being entertained and excited. Finally, Generation Z communicates best by smartphone with texts and social media.

In Susan's case, as described earlier, she might consider sending her manager (the Gen Xer) an email briefly noting the purpose for her wanting to meet with him and suggesting that his advice is valued and needed. When communicating with the human resources professional (Millennial), Susan might want to consider bringing her personal computer to the meeting with a brief PowerPoint presentation that outlines her career and experience and asking the HR representative's advice on career options that may be open for her in the company. Susan might also want to point out in the presentation those areas of interest and other positions that she might like to pursue.

Next, we list additional descriptions of each generation. Generational characteristics are not absolute and vary based on rural and urban settings, economic status, and early or late birth in each generation. People born three to five years on either side of each general date range given earlier are referred to as "cuspers" and may display characteristics of either or both of the generations.[2]

The Traditionalists: 1928–1945

- Currently make up less than 1 percent of the US workforce
- Most were children during World War II
- Raised in disciplined, nuclear families
- Embrace a strong sense of loyalty to their family, community, and country
- Committed team members and collaborators
- Place a strong emphasis on rules
- Lead with a "command and control" style
- Prefer face-to-face interaction but communicate best formally (e.g., memos)

Can you think of someone at work or in your family who might be a Traditionalist? Alex remembers working for a Traditionalist who always wanted a concise, one-page memo to review prior to meeting on any major subject or project.

Baby Boomers: 1946–1964

- Make up 27 percent of the US workforce, but their numbers are declining
- Childhood marked by the moon landing, the civil rights movement, President Kennedy's assassination, the Vietnam War, Woodstock, and the women's liberation movement
- Prefer to communicate in person in a direct and open style
- Known as the hardest-working generation, often prioritizing work over personal life
- Are retiring at a rate of ten thousand per day, but many can't afford to retire and want to work part-time
- Are inclined to seek contract work after retirement

Do you work with a Baby Boomer? Melissa did and recalls that her boss was a workaholic and required his leadership team to work on weekends as well. He wanted fast and direct information and gave fast and direct feedback.

Generation X: 1965–1980

- Make up 35 percent of the US workforce
- Childhood influenced by the energy crisis, Watergate, the AIDS epidemic, Chernobyl, and the fall of the Berlin Wall
- More independent, adaptable, and technically savvy than prior generations
- Question authority and prefer fewer rules
- Seek to balance work and family
- Want to communicate directly with leaders

Perhaps there is someone in your family who is a Gen Xer. Alex has two sons. Both are Gen X cuspers. They are independent and technically savvy and both have previously left positions in order to seek more freedom and latitude in their work. Both work hard at balancing work and family and, given their demanding positions, still succeed.

Millennials: 1981–1998

- Make up 37 percent of the US workforce now and are on track to constitute 46 percent of the workforce by 2020
- Childhood influenced by the Columbine shootings, 9/11, Enron, Hurricane Katrina, and, most important, the emergence of the internet
- Considered the most educated and diverse generation
- Tend to be energetic, technically savvy, and socially conscious
- Take an entrepreneurial approach to work
- Prefer direct communication and feedback
- Want a social, friendly work environment

Melissa has five Millennial children and stepchildren. All have college degrees, and four have advanced degrees. Three of them left their first job within one year because they didn't like the culture and work environment of their employer.

Generation Z: 1999–Present

- Make up 1–2 percent of the US workforce
- Are differentiated from Millennials, since Millennials are more focused on how situations will best benefit themselves, while Gen Zers seek to create their own balanced solutions
- Tend to be more entrepreneurial, cautious, and concerned with career stability
- First generation to grow up in a completely wireless world
- Considered to be hard working, ambitious, and innovative, with a desire to make a societal impact
- Communicate best by smartphone/texts/email and social media
- Have large networks but not much job experience; employers can leverage these networks[3]

When teaching at Rutgers Business School, the authors saw these characteristics in the freshman and sophomore students they taught. Students were very concerned about making sure they were educated to get a job; but at the same time, they were volunteers, and many worked in the community. Their smartphones were almost a body part.

Prior to sharing your life and career plan, seeking advice or help from a colleague, or going into a job interview, reflecting on the characteristics of the various age groups may help you to focus on the best way to get your message across and to achieve your goal.

One of the reasons why some thrive in the workplace while others struggle is because some people are able to adapt to other people ... better than others. The Kelly study reports that 72 percent of respondents said they adapt their communication when communicating with a coworker from a different generation.

—Chad Buleen, "How Do Age Differences Affect Business Communication?"

Morgan, a Millennial, liked the company she worked for and the position she held. However, she felt that the development programs offered by the company were not meeting her needs. Morgan had some options she wanted considered. She wanted to communicate directly with her boss, who she knew was a Gen Xer, a smart and cautious individual. Her normal communication style would be to simply walk into his office and start talking. She decided that sending an email would be the best way to get started. This would give her boss some time to think about her request. In the email, she asked for a meeting and stated why she wanted to talk to him and why it was important to her and the company. She asked a question: Would the company consider reimbursement of costs for courses or conferences applicable to her job? Morgan went into the meeting confident and ready. Her manager appreciated her candor and her directness. The meeting resulted in Morgan being given the okay to attend a major industry conference.

In addition, as you have learned earlier in this book, individuals are highly motivated by their personal values. So when seeking ways to connect and work with individuals across all generations, there are seven values that matter most to people of every age:

- Feeling respected
- Being listened to
- Having opportunities for mentoring
- Understanding the big picture
- Receiving effective communication
- Receiving positive feedback
- Experiencing an exchange of ideas[4]

Including some recognition of these values when meeting or communicating with others can be helpful. For example, you can listen intently, paint the big picture, be positive, and seek the other person's ideas or suggestions.

This review of the age groups in our workforce today is primarily meant to alert you that thinking about how you communicate with people is an important part of sharing your life and career plan and can also be used in interviews for a new position.

Cultural Intelligence

In addition to different age groups, organizations will also contain one or more cultures. A larger company might have a culture for each division, as well as an overarching corporate culture. A small business has its own culture. And the geographic community in which you work has a national, state, and local culture. Understanding something about the cultures in which you work can help you to communicate your desires in a way that makes the message more acceptable. Or, if you don't understand the culture around you, your message, delivered in the wrong way, could create a culture clash.

Important predictors of your success in today's world include not only your IQ, emotional intelligence, résumé, or expertise but also your cultural intelligence (CQ). This powerful ability is something anyone can learn and is proven to enhance your effectiveness when working in culturally diverse situations. Research conducted in more than thirty countries has shown that people with high CQ are better able to adjust and adapt to the unpredictable, complex situations of life and work in today's globalized world.[5]

It may be counterintuitive, but individuals who never have lived abroad or traveled very much but are engaged with people of different cultures, even in the same nation, can develop a high degree of CQ. Although it is helpful to have lived or worked in different cultures around the world, it is not necessary to develop a high degree of CQ.[6]

The reactions that people have to you can be driven by their culture, just as your culture can drive your reaction to others. They may think something like the following: "This person is like me." "He really is pushy, isn't he?" "She is so quiet." "This person doesn't know how to dress for an interview." "When she talked about her accomplishments, she seemed rather arrogant." This type of thinking is a reflection of how individuals see you in relation to their cultural expectations. For example, someone might think that a man who doesn't wear a tie is not dressed for an interview or that if he wears a tie, he is too formal or overdressed for an interview. One's organizational culture could dictate either of these responses. Or one might have an expectation that individuals should be humble and not brag about achievements because of the way one's parents decided to educate their children in their family culture.

Individuals in some cultures learn to respect one another by working together over a long term. Individuals in other cultures get right down to business and don't wait to make friends. Recognizing the culture of the individual you are dealing with and the culture in which you are operating can present an advantage as you move toward accomplishing the goals you set for yourself in your life and career plan.

Intercultural intelligence or competence is generally defined as the ability to communicate and behave in appropriate ways with those who are culturally different from you. In addition, it includes the ability to develop shared spaces, teams, and organizations that are inclusive, effective, innovative, and satisfying.[7]

In business, your skills in identifying and understanding cultural differences are critical to choosing the appropriate strategy. There are more than two hundred different national cultures in the world. Richard D. Lewis has separated them into three main cultural types:

- Multi-active. Described as warm, emotional, loquacious, and impulsive. This includes people from countries like Brazil, Chile, Argentina, and Mexico.
- Linear-active. Described as cool, factual, and decisive in planning. This includes countries like the United States, Germany, Switzerland, Luxembourg, and Great Britain.
- Reactive. Described as courteous, amiable, accommodating, willing to compromise, and good at listening. This includes countries like Japan, China, Vietnam, and South Korea.[8]

The following chart describes key characteristics or traits of the three main cultural types.

Three Cultural Types

Multi-active	Linear-active	Reactive
Values family	Values facts	Uses intuition
Respects hierarchy	Values planning	Values honor
Values human relations	Is very results oriented	Invests in meaningful
Engages in rhetoric	Desires punctuality	relations
Values loyalty	Keeps word	Values duty and
Speaks all the time	Has trust in institutions	responsibility
Has many jobs at once	Has trust in the law	Desires harmony
Does not value planning	Speaks to the point	Values and preserves
as much	Is focused on one task	reputation
Shows emotions	Is consistent in approach	Values politeness
Has many excuses	Talks straight but is	Avoids straight contact
Frequently interrupts or	polite	Listens all the time
stops discussion	Is sometimes emotional	Hides emotions
Values emotions over	Does not like to lose face	Is not confrontational
facts	Tries not to interrupt	Values diplomacy over
Has flexible truth	when listening	the truth
	Values truth	Cannot lose face
		Never interrupts

A growing number of individuals and organizations are discovering the competitive edge that comes from enhancing CQ. Scientific research reveals that these are the most predictable results expected from increasing your cultural intelligence:

- Superior cross-cultural adjustment. Most twenty-first-century interests and jobs require adjustment to various cultures. Cultural intelligence has more to do with your success in multicultural endeavors than do your age, gender, location, or IQ.
- Improved job performance. Individuals with a higher CQ also have an edge in a competitive job market. Even if a position doesn't require any international travel, managers and human resources departments are realizing the importance of having culturally astute employees who can meet the challenges of serving a diverse

customer base at home and abroad, as well as becoming meaningful participants of culturally diverse teams.

- Enhanced personal well-being. Enhancing your cultural intelligence is shown to enhance your personal satisfaction and overall well-being, particularly when engaging in culturally diverse situations.
- Greater profitability. There is also a connection between CQ and profitability. Individuals who more successfully adjust cross-culturally and who perform better in essential tasks such as decision-making, negotiations, and networking help their organizations save and earn more money. Many executives see the benefits of hiring, promoting, and rewarding individuals with high CQ. On average, individuals with higher CQ earn more.[9]

When Alex became the president of American Field Service (AFS), he had chief executive officer responsibility for the entire company. AFS was the nation's largest student-exchange organization, exchanging students between the United States and fifty other countries. All of the company's functions reported to Alex, as the CEO, and he, in turn, reported to a board of directors. The mission of the company was to provide experiences that would increase international and intercultural learning for individuals, families, and schools. In his role, Alex engaged with individuals from many different countries, and it took him at least a year or two to realize he was bringing a very US-centered approach to the work. He was behaving and working in ways that were completely acceptable in the United States but did not always correlate with the way his global partners wanted to work. That approach created clashes with colleagues from other nations who approached their work differently from the way he approached his. For example, some individuals from Latin cultures wanted to build friendships based on warmth and spending time together before getting down to what really needed to get done. Individuals from Asian cultures did not engage publicly as much as people from other cultures did and at times were concerned about saving face, not being embarrassed, and developing a relationship that was time based—the longer the time, the better the relationship. Individuals from northern

European countries wanted to get right to the point of what had to get done to achieve the goal. Although Alex did experience these characteristics from the people he worked with, we don't want you to read these comments as a broad-brush generalization of what all individuals from those countries are like. All people in a particular nation and society are not exactly the same in their behavior. However, one does need to be conscious of those intercultural parameters that may be under the surface in any relationship. Intercultural competence is, in essence, about communicating with people clearly and avoiding misunderstandings. Intercultural training helps people appreciate how culture may impact communication with their colleagues or clients. Training, education, and assessment in intercultural competence are available to individuals who have an interest. (See the listed resources at the end of the book.)

Strength lies in differences, not in similarities.

—Stephen R. Covey, *The 7 Habits of Highly Effective People*

When your life and career plan is completed and you begin to deploy it, think about the age groups and cultural positioning of the individuals to whom you are going to talk about your plan.

- Would it be better to start the conversation with an email or text invitation?
- Would going to lunch be helpful or a hindrance?
- Should you prepare material to provide to the individual in advance, or should you hand it to the person when you meet?
- Are you adept at bringing up subject matter important to that individual's age or culture?
- How does your own positioning in your age group or culture impact you?
- Will that affect the way you communicate?

Carlos, one of our clients, told us about a business meeting that included business representatives from Japan, Sweden, France, Costa Rica, Brazil, and the United States. Carlos had a great deal of intercultural acumen. He explained that the group was engaged in trying to resolve a key business challenge that was caused by the actions of their Japanese partner. As they began to seek common ground, the French participant pointed out that the problem they had was all because of actions taken by their Japanese partner. He began to criticize the Japanese representative in front of everyone. This caused a great deal of public embarrassment for the Japanese representative, who had difficulty in accepting and processing the feedback. After some additional conversation among the members, Carlos recognized that coming to an agreement that day was going to be next to impossible, so he suggested a break in the proceedings and a continuation of the meeting the next day. In the meantime, he talked to the French representative, explaining the problem that had developed. The French representative met privately with the representative from Japan and apologized. The following day, he also apologized to the group for taking it off track and for placing the Japanese representative in a difficult position. This allowed the group to begin their problem-solving process again by focusing on the problem and not blame.

Now that you are somewhat more cognizant of the types of differences discussed in this chapter, give some thought to them before launching into the actions noted in your plan. The key is to be in a position where you are putting your best foot forward by communicating and behaving in a way that is acceptable to the individuals with whom you will meet.

The human diversity impacting all of us continues to grow. The individual who deals with diversity appropriately and takes advantage of it demonstrates a powerful strength.

—Alex J. Plinio

What Have You Learned by Considering Different Age Groups and Cultures?

_____

_____

_____

_____

_____

_____

_____

_____

Ideas for My Action Plan

1. _____

2. _____

3. _____

4. _____

All of your good work on your life and career plan is meant to lead you to a place that is satisfying, comfortable, and fulfilling. That place is your personal vision. It is where you want to arrive at some specific point in time. And when you arrive, that place will have maximum potential to bring you happiness.

PART III

Putting It All Together

Using All Aspects of Your Self, Work, and Career to Create a Future That You Can Plan and Work Toward

CHAPTER 12

Personal Vision

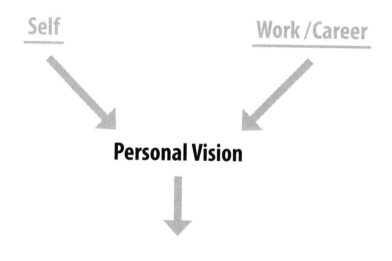

The purpose of this chapter is to help you to think about what your life and career will look like at some future date, thereby creating a destination at which you hope to arrive and in which self-satisfaction and happiness are attained.

Most individuals have an easier time thinking about what the next month or year might be like for them. It gets a bit more difficult when peering into a future that could be three, five, or ten years from now. For some people, it's hard to do this since we are asking our mind to picture a state of life that's quite intangible in the present time. However, just as a company or organization develops its vision, individuals are no less in need of knowing what their future is expected to look like. There are all kinds of sayings that are appropriate to this point. "If you don't know where you're going, you will never know when you arrive." "A ship that's not steered lands anywhere." "If you don't know where you're going, when you reach a fork in the road, you won't know which way to turn." " Yesterday is gone, today is a new day, and tomorrow can be our invention." In other words, having a vision can be a decision-making tool.

For example, Cindy was recruited by a firm that wanted to hire her for a position similar to her current job, only at higher compensation. When she referred to her life and career plan and the personal vision she had developed, she saw that by remaining in her current firm, she could attain a vice president position sooner, which was a key goal in her plan and the position that she wanted within the time frame painted in her vision. This made Cindy much more comfortable in foregoing a higher compensation today for the position she desired in her vision.

Jerry was retiring soon. His plan called for spending time traveling with his wife, being with his grandchildren, and coaching Little League baseball, among other things. His employer approached him and asked if he would consider working two or three days a week as a consultant after he left his job. Jerry's life and career plan proved that he had sufficient funds for his retirement and didn't need to work. And working longer, even part-time, wasn't part of his personal vision. He decided to do what would make him happy and said no to his employer.

Not only is a personal vision a tool to be deployed for decision-making, but it is also aspirational and motivational and becomes a driving force when reviewed on a periodic basis. Your vision can be shared with others in order to demonstrate that you have thought about and made decisions about where you want to take your life. This is especially helpful when seeking mentoring from trusted individuals. Although it may not be possible to achieve 100 percent of your personal vision, even the achievement of 70, 80, or 90 percent of your vision can be extremely satisfying. It may not be possible to get everything you want. However, without a vision, and without trying, it would be nearly impossible to get what you want.

The biggest adventure you can take is to live the life of your dreams.

—Oprah Winfrey

It may help to think in a more picturesque fashion about your future. So let's say that your life to date is a car driving on a specific road. That road falls behind you. In front of you is the road that you're going to be traveling in the future. It includes all the choices and decisions you will make as you drive your life forward. When you deploy your life and career plan, it becomes the engine to drive you down that road. Farther in the distance there's a hill that turns into a mountain, and at the top of the mountain is your personal vision. That vision depicts what things will look like for you when you arrive. You may be a young person early in your career and without a lot of experience. Therefore you may choose to look out only three or four years into the future. So your arrival destination for your life and career plan would be three or four years from now. Of course, when you arrive at that destination, you will need to develop a new life and career plan by revising your current plan and developing a new vision. If you're a person in midcareer, you may want to use your life experience to look out a little further, maybe five or six years, thereby basing your personal vision on how things might look at that point in your life. A person could be very near retirement and not have thought very much about planning for the future. Instead, this individual should focus his or her vision on the last year of work followed by the first two years of retirement in order to create a bridge to a new way of life. That new life might include some or no paid work, volunteerism, free leisure time, consulting, and travel.

Things change fairly rapidly throughout our lives, and although one could go out ten years or more to envision what one's life might be like, we suggest that you focus on a three- to five-year vision to start.

Luca was a young manager who was developing her life and career plan when she found out she was pregnant. In this special circumstance, she had to consider a number of things, including how long she would work until the birth of her child, when or even if she would return to work, whether this was the start of a larger family, and what the impact would be on her financial plans. Luca's personal vision had been three years out and included a job promotion. She thought that her pregnancy would delay the promotion, so she changed her vision and concluded that she did want to return to work six months after the birth of her child. Her plan was for more time at home with her family. Her financial plan changed as well, since she now expected her promotion to take place one year later than originally planned.

Regardless of the place in life that you're in, the ground rules for creating a personal vision are the same.

- First, think about your life as the road you have traveled, and consider where you are now.
- Second, look forward down the road, up the hill, and to the top of the mountain. Picture yourself having traveled that road, whether it is three or five years from now.
- Third, describe what you see at the top of the mountain.

Document what you see in a sufficient amount of detail. For example, for your career, note the type of position you will have, the type of organization you will be working in, the amount of expected compensation and benefits, the culture of the organization in which you will be working, the type of work you will be doing, the kind of relationships you expect to have, the geographic area in which you will work, and so on. Also include a description of your life-work balance—how you spend the minutes, hours, days of your life at that point. Will you be cultivating your interests? What are they? What aspects of your life will be providing joy? What is the impact of this new stage of your life on your personal mission statement and values? Have there been any changes in your personal relationships and family? What are they? Does your current work position place you on the correct path to achieve your vision? Most important, if you imagine yourself stepping back and taking a look at the personal vision that you are writing now, which describes some time in the future, if you were actually there, would it make you feel satisfied and happy that you have arrived in that place?

Your vision will become clear only when you look into your heart. Who looks outside, dreams. Who looks inside, awakens.

—Carl Jung

The road that you are going to travel to your personal vision may not always be straight. It may have side streets down which you are forced to venture. For example, you're squarely on the road toward your vision, and you suddenly lose your job. In the short term, you may have to take a new position that takes you off your main path. It may not be the right "next job" for your personal vision. Or illness rather than job loss derails you. No matter what occurs, keep trying to find your way back to your main path. The important thing to keep in mind is that if you know where the road is leading and recognize which events happening in your life will slow you down or move you off your road, you should be able to find your way back. If you cannot find your way back to your original vision path, if circumstances have changed in your life that substantially, you need to develop a new road to a new personal vision as a result of life's events, and that means developing a revised life and career plan.

Consider this vision statement developed by Nicholas, a human resources manager, using a five-year horizon. Nicholas graduated from college and worked for two different employers over a ten-year period and then arrived at his current employer. He was recently promoted to human resources manager after completing his life and career plan, which included the following vision statement.

My Personal Five-Year Vision: What I Believe Things Will Look Like in Five Years

I am the vice president of human resources for a midsize corporation. I obtained this position after spending three years as a human resources manager. With the support of my company, I also went back to school and earned an MBA with an emphasis on human resources. I report to the CEO of the corporation and have a positive and productive working relationship with that person. My HR team is highly regarded within the organization, and we are known for being responsive, fair ambassadors for the corporate culture. I am challenged, productive, and fulfilled in my role as head of HR.

My wife and two children are supportive of my career. I do put in full days because of my leadership role, but I have a highly functioning team at work and am able to eat dinner with the family on most nights. My weekends are usually free, and our family enjoys going on camping trips. We have taken sailing lessons and now own a Sunfish sailboat that we dock at a nearby lake. My wife and I participate in local 5k races and enjoy exercising together most mornings. My wife and I also belong to a dinner club group and enjoy an active social life. My energetic lifestyle allows me to regularly engage with my family and supports a healthy way of life that keeps me fit and feeling my best. We vacation for at least two weeks annually.

I experience joy in my life through my interests, family, work associates, and staying healthy. My personal values, which include independence, teamwork, life balance, and personal accountability, can be actualized at the present time.

My financial compensation is sufficient to support my current lifestyle. However, I can see I must seek additional compensation in order to assure the future education of my children and the eventual purchase of a second home. Other than our mortgage, we have no debt. This makes me feel good.

Two years ago my wife and I met with a financial planner to develop our first financial plan. I wish we had done it earlier. However, in implementing the plan, I have a very good feeling that we can achieve our goals for our family and for eventual retirement.

The vision statement developed by Nicholas shows where he is going and where he wants to arrive in five years. He has looked back at his life and career, assessed where he currently is, and created a vivid picture of what he wants his life to be in five years.

A well-thought-out vision can help individuals manage the change in their life. It connects their mission and their values to their future state. It helps individuals to be the leader of their lives, leading in a direction they have chosen. It can be transformative. Developing your vision is a journey helping you to learn what you believe a successful life looks like. It aligns the key ingredients in your life so that they can powerfully push you forward from the present to the future. The vision is a roadmap to your desired state.

I visualized where I wanted to be, what kind of player I wanted to become. I knew exactly where I wanted to go, and I focused on getting there.

—Michael Jordan

In the book *Built to Last*, Jim Collins and Jerry Porras state, "We selected the phrase 'envision the future' recognizing that it contains a paradox. On the one hand, it conveys a sense of concreteness—something vivid and real; you can see, touch it, feel it. On the other hand, it portrays a time yet unrealized—a dream, hope, or aspiration." They go on to say that "a vivid description is a vibrant, engaging, and specific description of what it will be like to achieve" the vision. "Think of it as translating the vision from words into pictures, of creating an image that people can carry around in their heads."[1]

Let's get started on your own vision statement. Picture yourself three, four, or five years from now. Put in as much detail as you can. Describe what life and work will be like. Close your eyes and dream, and then open your eyes and look inside yourself. Try to include in your vision statement something from each part of the Life & Career Planning Model that we have explored in the book.

My Personal Vision Statement

_____

_____

_____

_____

_____

_____

_____

_____

_____

_____

_____

_____

_____

_____

_____

_____

_____

_____

After having worked through the chapters in this book, you now know where you are in your life and career, and by building your personal vision, you know where you want to end up at a specific point in time. The important thing is to determine how you are going to get there. You're going to get there by having a strong life and career plan and activating it. The actions in the plan will lead to the achievement of your interim goals, which power you to the next stop along the road to your vision.

A vision is not just a picture of what could be; it is an appeal to our better selves, a call to become something more.

—Rosabeth Moss Kanter, professor of business at Harvard Business School, management consultant, author

What Have You Learned by Developing Your Personal Vision?

_____

_____

_____

_____

_____

_____

_____

_____

_____

Ideas for My Action Plan

1. _____

2. _____

3. _____

4. _____

You have turned the corner. Now is the time to analyze the work you have done and to glean all of the insights that you can. With this information, you can then embark on building a strong life and career plan.

CHAPTER 13

Analysis and Learning

Personal Vision

Analysis and Learning

The purpose of this chapter is to analyze your work so far and determine the insights that have been derived from your planning process. It will also help you to explore potential opportunities and actions revealed as a result of your lessons learned. Finally, you may pick up themes that repeat across parts of the model, some of which could be disturbing and need attention. The output from this chapter becomes input for your plan.

If you have come this far, you have done some great work with the Life & Career Planning Model by working through the various chapters of the book. You are now on the downhill slope. Let's get started by analyzing what you have accomplished so far and documenting your lessons so that we can place them directly into your action plan.

As you went through each part of the model, you should have written down the important findings and lessons that you discerned from your hard work. In some cases, you might have noted actions that might be required or some changes that you might need to make to adjust your situation. So let's start with a review of your answers to all the parts of the model and document in one place these findings, potential changes, and actions needed. We also need to look for similar themes or repeating answers that you gave across different parts of the model. These themes are contained in your previously documented responses to the various questions and exercises you responded to and completed throughout the book. Finally, we must determine if there are opportunities to consider in your current situation. To start your thinking and to get your juices flowing, we think it would be helpful to begin by documenting your responses to the following questions:

- What are the major lessons you learned about yourself by using this model?

_____

_____

_____

- How do your interests, the things that give you joy, and your personal values intersect with one another?

_____

_____

_____

- What does your work on the model tell you about your current relationships? Are any of them toxic? Which have the most meaning for you?

_____

_____

_____

- Does your current life balance reflect who you want to be and how you want to live your life?

_____

_____

_____

- Are you in a personal and professional position to be able to achieve your life's purpose?

_____

_____

_____

- Are you going to be able to achieve your desired career outcomes where you work now? If not, what are you going to do? What are your options?

_____

_____

_____

- Are there areas of your own personal or career development that you must focus on?

_____

_____

_____

- Do you have a financial plan? If not, when will you have one?

_____

_____

_____

- Describe your current work environment. Are you relatively happy? Do you like your job?

_____

_____

_____

- Does your job impact your personal life, including your relationships with family and friends, the way that you want it to? Are you making enough money? Do you have enough free time?

_____

_____

_____

- What are the key themes in your life?

_____

_____

_____

- What is disturbing, uncomfortable, or even scary about your current life situation? Why is it disturbing? Are you willing to do something about your situation so that it is no longer disturbing?

_____

_____

_____

- Currently in your life and career, do you see any opportunities? What makes it an opportunity? Can you be opportunistic and take advantage of it?

_____

_____

_____

- What are you hiding that needs to be brought into the light?

_____

_____

_____

- What next steps do you need to take to help you prepare for success?

_____

_____

_____

So, at the end of each section of the model, when you considered things that could impact your plan and noted any potential actions you could take, you were building substance to be used to develop your plan. By going back and reviewing what you thought at the time and bringing that information forward, you will have the start of the action items that should permeate your plan.

Here are a couple of possible examples:

- You described several interests that are important to you, and yet you admit that you don't take the time to develop those interests or to enjoy them as much as you would like. What can you do about this?
- You explored your personal values and found that you have a values conflict—perhaps with a friend or relative or maybe on the job. What can you do about this?
- You discovered that you really don't have a key relationship with anyone with whom you are willing to share your thoughts or discuss your plans. Or you do have an important relationship, but instead of it being a key one, it is toxic for you. What can be done about this?
- You found that your time at work is excessive, and your home life is suffering. What can you do?
- You feel good that you are taking care of your health, but you worry about taking on more responsibilities at work and what impact it might have on your health and your life balance. What will you do?
- You had a tough time working on the section of the model about your life's purpose, but you did it; and now when you look at your

job, interests, and values, you see some conflicts. What needs to be done?

- You know there are areas of your performance that need bolstering or improvement. What steps, if any, will you take?
- After you described the type of future position you desire, you saw that it is possible to get that position where you are currently employed. What steps will you take?
- Your vision statement excites you because of the possibilities it describes. But it also scares you since the future it promises seems far away or difficult to attain. How will you proceed?

These few examples of how to question your responses to the steps of the model are typical of the reactions students and clients have when they perform this exercise. Of course, there are many more ways to approach gathering your thoughts about the various action steps you will need to take, and you will most likely have found some responses both similar to and different from those just described. That's good, because you need to decide what can be done to fix what is wrong with your current situation, retain what is right with your life, and seek new opportunities at the same time.

Man's mind, once stretched by a new idea, never regains its original dimensions.

—Oliver Wendell Holmes

Now let's move from the generic examples just presented to a more specific and personal example. Start by using the documentation you prepared at the end of each model topic and your answers to the suggested ways of questioning just presented above. These are the initial fodder for the actions to be documented in your plan. For each section of the model, start writing down what you previously recorded as lessons learned and potential actions. In addition, document any special observations and potential opportunities that you see. As an example, you can do it like this:

Interests

Lessons:

Observations:

Potential Actions:

Potential Opportunities:

Example:

Lessons: I love to exercise at my gym. It is a passion of mine, but I don't get to do it often enough.

Observation: I work late almost every weekday and too many Saturdays. Frankly I'm tired.

Potential Actions: Leave work earlier at least one day during the week and get to the gym. Reduce the number of Saturdays worked and get to the gym. Calendar in time at the gym with friends.

Potential Opportunities: Get a personal trainer to help me.

Don't worry about the fact that you haven't figured out how to reduce your work hours. We will get to that in the action plan. For now, just state what you must do to achieve your goal of getting to the gym more often.

Joy

Lessons:

Observations:

Potential Actions:

Potential Opportunities:

Example:

Lessons: Certain aspects of my work have given me joy, such as leading teams, while in my personal life, being with family and friends in social settings is how I like to spend my time.

Observations: I need to think about how I can participate more in teams at work, and I have to take more of the initiative to gather together family and friends for social reasons.

Potential Actions: Seek more team positions or team leadership roles. Set up a calendar of social activity that I initiate at least once every month or so.

Potential Opportunities: There's a new product being developed at my company; see if I can get on the launch team. My wife's birthday is in June; plan a surprise party.

Now you fill in your own answers to the various parts of the model in the same way, using your own lessons, observations, and potential actions and opportunities and referring back to your previous documentation as needed.

Interests

Lessons: _____

_____

_____

Observations: _____

_____

_____

Potential Actions: _____

_____

_____

Potential Opportunities: _____

_____

_____

Joy

Lessons: _____

_____

_____

Observations: _____

_____

_____

Potential Actions: _____

_____

_____

Potential Opportunities: _____

_____

_____

Personal Values

Lessons: _____

_____

_____

Observations: _____

_____

_____

Potential Actions: _____

_____

_____

Potential Opportunities: _____

_____

_____

Relationships

Lessons: _____

_____

_____

Observations: _____

_____

_____

Potential Actions: _____

_____

_____

Potential Opportunities: _____

_____

_____

Life Mission/Purpose

Lessons: _____

_____

_____

Observations: _____

_____

_____

Potential Actions: _____

_____

_____

Potential Opportunities: _____

_____

_____

Life Balance

Lessons: _____

_____

_____

Observations: _____

_____

_____

Potential Actions: _____

_____

_____

Potential Opportunities: _____

_____

_____

Strengths and Development Areas

Lessons: _____

_____

_____

Observations: _____

_____

_____

Potential Actions: _____

_____

_____

Potential Opportunities: _____

_____

_____

Organizational Culture, Mission and Values

Lessons: _____

_____

_____

Observations: _____

_____

_____

Potential Actions: _____

_____

_____

Potential Opportunities: _____

_____

_____

Financial Plans

Lessons: _____

_____

_____

Observations: _____

_____

_____

Potential Actions: _____

_____

_____

Potential Opportunities: _____

_____

_____

Current and Future Positions

Lessons: _____

_____

_____

Observations: _____

_____

_____

Potential Actions: _____

_____

_____

Potential Opportunities: _____

_____

_____

Crossing Age Groups and Cultures

Lessons: _____

_____

_____

Observations: _____

_____

_____

Potential Actions: _____

_____

_____

Potential Opportunities: _____

_____

_____

Vision

Lessons: _____

_____

_____

Observations: _____

_____

_____

Potential Actions: _____

_____

_____

Potential Opportunities: _____

_____

_____

If you have gone through all the various areas and thought about what you've learned and observed and located a few opportunities to take advantage of as well as actions you can take to improve your situation, you have done a lot of good work here. This will help your planning immensely. Now, let's reflect a bit on what you've found.

When reviewing all of this data, what are the most important areas calling for action in your life? For example, you find that your most pressing need is to find a job matching your values and vision. Or your family is important to you, but you find you are not spending the time needed with your children. Or you realize that you want to do work that contributes to society. Write these most prevalent areas down in the emerging themes box below.

Andrew was an entry-level executive in a midsized company. He was in his midfifties, had a family, and had a comfortable financial life. When he went through this exercise as one of our clients, Andrew realized that he suffered from overcommitment. He saw that his life was not in balance since he had taken on a great deal of overtime work, which was cutting into his personal life. He felt like he was becoming a workaholic. In addition, he also found that he had a hard time saying no to requests for help whether from friends, family, or organizations for which he volunteered. He noted that as a result of the decisions he was making regarding work, his relationships, and his areas of interest, he was inadvertently placing a great deal of stress on himself, and this began to affect other areas of his life as well. For instance, he had gained thirty pounds over the past year and had given up going to the gym on a regular basis. At work, he, more than his superiors, was making the decision to work extra hours, while at home, he was spending less time with his wife and children. He recognized that he was not thinking about his long-term potential and was too focused on his present situation.

As you look at your own lessons, observations, and potential actions, you too will see some themes emerging. These themes are areas calling for action and can be seen in several of the parts of the model. They should stand out for you. List them below.

Emerging Themes

1. _____

2. _____

3. _____

4. _____

5. _____

6. _____

7. _____

Now, let's think about potential opportunities currently at your doorstep. Sometimes people can immediately sense the opportunities in their current environment, while others need prodding in order to see them.

For example, Judy was in her current position at a large manufacturing company for seven years. Her compensation increases were very modest, and her promotions were infrequent. She liked her company and the work that she was doing with purchasing and order processing, but overall she was not happy.

However, Judy was reluctant to follow up on a coworker's suggestion to consider current job openings at their workplace. Judy was an individual who had a fairly low tolerance for risk and felt that it was safer to stay where she was, with the job she had. However, after completing the Life & Career Planning Model, she recognized that she was limiting herself. Not only should she take recommendations from friends about other positions, especially since she wasn't very happy in the job she currently held, but she herself needed to ferret out new positions at her current employer and not be afraid to seek what she wanted. This insight led her to have discussions inside the company while also creating a personal marketing plan, which she launched using her network and a social media job-search site to begin a process of determining just what was out there for her.

So let's start a creative process that will get us thinking about potential opportunities for you. When you completed the various steps in the model, you learned certain things that we can use now to identify opportunities. How do you feel about your current position? What was it you had to say about your next or future position? Is there an opportunity right now where you work to seek that future position? What must you do and to whom should you talk to develop that opportunity? When thinking about your relationships, you may have noted that your network was not as robust as it needed to be. Can you begin to contact the people in your network about opportunities that they might see for you while at the same time asking your contacts for the names of additional people who might help you to identify specific opportunities in the future?

It's time to be the leader of your life. It's time to take your life in the direction you want to take it.

Joan, a forty-five-year-old executive in her company at the vice president level, was divorced with no children. After going through the Life & Career Planning Model, she realized that she wanted to be able to establish a very strong emotional relationship with a man that could eventually lead to marriage once again. When she realized that this was a very legitimate desire she had, we asked her to put together a marketing plan for herself. Many opportunities can arise if you start from the assumption that *you* are the product that you want to sell. After we fully discussed this with her, she did develop a marketing plan that included such things as using her networks of friends and associates to introduce her to people, joining social media sites, and letting it be known among her churchgoing friends that she wanted to meet someone to date again. When she reported back to us three months later, she had been on nearly fifty dates, most for short periods of time—coffee, lunch, or a drink. She then narrowed down the relationships she was forming to six or seven people who were of long-term interest. Eighteen months later, Joan was engaged to be married. She had created the opportunity that she sought.

Today I meet people who do not identify with the word leader. They say, "I'm not the boss. I can't do that." In the military, I learned that leadership is not about positional authority; it's all about behaviors.

—Sean Lynch, senior consultant for Lead Star

Okay, let's get started with you. List between three and five opportunities that emerged from the analysis, lessons, and observations you have made so far. What are they? When we get to the action plan stage of the model, we will talk more about these. However, for now please do the following: for each of the potential opportunities, state at least two potential actions for each one to be considered more concretely when you get to the action planning stage. Don't censor yourself. Even if something sounds impossible or difficult, list the potential actions anyway if they can help you get to your stated goals. Do that now.

Opportunities

1. _____

    Action 1 _____

    Action 2 _____

2. _____

    Action 1 _____

    Action 2 _____

3. _____

    Action 1 _____

    Action 2 _____

4. _____

    Action 1 _____

    Action 2 _____

5. _____

    Action 1 _____

    Action 2 _____

Considering all of your analysis, let's focus on what may be scaring the heck out of you. Alex recalls that in one of his graduate-level classes, during a discussion about personal and organizational values, a woman, probably forty years of age or so, told the class that she was aware that she had, for some time, had a values conflict at work. She described being treated poorly by her supervisors in very demeaning ways. When asked whether she had approached her supervisors or someone in the human resources department or anyone else in the company about this situation, she said she had not. She was concerned that if she did, she might lose her job. Finally, she looked for another job and left the organization. This terrible treatment by her manager had been going on for seven years. It was a bad time economically to move, and she was afraid to move ahead on finding a position. Here is a person afraid to face a key issue at work and afraid to face an external environment to seek a new job. That fear cost her seven years of her life in worry and abuse. Some of you reading this book may be in similar positions. If something scares you, it is a barrier, and it must be surmounted. The actions that you produce are the key for you to be able to move ahead. They will help you, along with support from your key relationships, to build up the courage to get done what has to get done.

Doug, for example, was an executive in a top firm. He had a lovely family, a highly compensated position, two homes, and all of those attributes one might expect from an individual who was a very good leader and had attained a great deal in his personal and work life. Doug wanted to achieve more in his professional life. He was looking for his next-level position. In his case, this would be a high-level executive role reporting to a chief executive officer.

While Alex was coaching him, Doug was in the final stages of interviewing with two separate companies for the type of role he sought. The positions were a bit different, but either one was certainly acceptable to him. It became evident to Alex that Doug was somewhat reluctant to move toward one of the jobs, being a bit afraid of the responsibilities and the new learning required. In one of the discussions, Alex asked Doug, "Which of these two jobs, which compensate similarly and both of which you would enjoy, scares the hell out of you?" Doug looked at Alex quizzically, and Alex said, "Doug, why would I ask you such a question?" "Because," Doug said, "you want me to get at what might stop me from saying yes to that job." Alex said, "That's correct, but also, one of these positions will challenge you more, will produce more learning and personal and professional growth, and once you've conquered that job, you will have a whole set of new experiences in your bag of tricks and on your résumé. Since both jobs are fairly equal, choose to overcome your fear."

Let's look at your own themes and lessons, and let's choose three or four things that make you feel disturbed, uncomfortable, or perhaps even fearful. Remember, it is a strength, not a weakness, to recognize and admit that some things may scare you. If you don't have the courage to name that thing, it will remain with you and impede your progress.

- Do you have a toxic relationship with someone that has to end?
- Do you have a job that you have to leave?
- Will you get to the gym more often and spend less time at work regardless of what people think?
- Do you need to spend time building key relationships and a network?
- Have you avoided asking for that compensation increase?
- After looking at your financial plan, are you afraid that you are not going to be able to meet your future retirement goals?
- You know that it will take time to gain knowledge about the financial aspects of the business you are in and you need that for promotion, but are you concerned about returning to school?
- Your lifestyle hasn't been as healthy as it needs to be, but can you take enough time to take care of yourself?
- Did your purpose or mission statement scare you because it pointed you in the direction of a complete career change?

Once you've listed up to five of these items that make you uncomfortable or prevent you from taking action right now, think about at least two actions that you might take to overcome these roadblocks. List them on the following page.

Things That Disturb Me

1. _____

   Action 1 _____

   Action 2 _____

2. _____

   Action 1 _____

   Action 2 _____

3. _____

   Action 1 _____

   Action 2 _____

4. _____

   Action 1 _____

   Action 2 _____

5. _____

   Action 1 _____

   Action 2 _____

If you don't know where you are going, you'll end up someplace else.

—Yogi Berra

What Have You Learned during Your Analysis of Your Lessons Learned?

In this chapter, you have brought together many ideas and potential actions for your life and career plan. Each part of the model and your documentation and everything you have recorded in this chapter are the inputs to developing your plan.

In the next chapter, we will be focused on your plan, your actions, and your future. So now is the time to take one last look at your documentation for each of the parts of the model that you have completed. As you go though your notes and each of the questions asked and examples provided, if you want to make any changes, now is the time to do that. You have come a long way, so let's move toward the payoff.

CHAPTER 14

Planning, Action, and Renewal

Draft
Plan

Share and
Test

Repeat

The Plan

Renewal

Action

The purpose of this chapter is to assimilate all of your good work and thoughtful preparation into an action plan that will propel you onto a path to your best life. In addition, we will make recommendations for the use of your plan and the model for the rest of your life.

Hopefully your diligent efforts have taught you something not only about yourself but also about where you are at the present time in your life and career and where you want to go. To translate your learning and insights into an actionable plan, you will have to think about and review the work that you have done. Use the potential action charts you completed at the end of each chapter and review the lessons you documented. Also focus on both the things that disturb you the most and current opportunities.

You have been given a gift—your life. What will you do with it?

—**Michael Hyatt,** *Living Forward*

The Plan

First, how far in advance do you want to plan? We recommend that you look ahead at least two years but no more than three years. The reason for this is that things have a way of changing with a level of rapidity we can seldom predict—you lose a job, you obtain a new job, a child is born, illness strikes someone in the family, a new home is purchased, and on and on. For the purposes of this chapter, we are going to focus on a plan looking out two years to get you started.

Next, you need to force yourself to concentrate on a discrete number of strategies, probably no more than six to eight per year. A strategy is a stated plan of action designed to achieve a major aim for a desired future, so you have to be specific about what you want to achieve. You don't want to overwhelm yourself or to be unrealistic in choosing just how much you believe you can accomplish.

Third, specific goals will need to be established for each of your strategies. A goal is the object of your effort, a desired result that you commit to achieve. To make your plan effective, the goals must be specific, measurable wherever possible, attainable and realistic, and time based. To begin the planning process, you need to look back at the work you have done on your life and career plan and begin to make choices about the areas of strategic focus that are most important to you now. As a model or a possible approach for doing this, we have noted below a simple way to assimilate information that one can then develop into strategies, for which goals can be stated.

My Strategic Focus

Model topic	Insights	Strategy	Goals and time line
Life balance	Although my life balance is in fairly good shape, I'm not spending enough time cultivating my friendships. It's important for me to expand and deepen my friendships.	Identify current friends and potential new friends for cultivating and deepening relationships.	1. Beginning in February, contact six friends and set up a poker club for a once-a-month game. 2. Identify someone at work and someone in my neighborhood who I believe could become a good friend. Invite the person to lunch to get acquainted by the end of the month. 3. Make better use of email, texting, and social media to find out what my friends are up to and to let them know more about me. Use photos for the first time on social media. Do this weekly. 4. In six months, evaluate whether I have made more friends, have deepened relationships with friends, and am comfortable with the amount of time I spend with my friends.

Model topic	Insights	Strategy	Goals and time line
Current and future position	Although I might be able to achieve my career goals in my current organization, I am not 100 percent sure of this. I may need to leave to get what I want out of my life and career.	In my current workplace, seek the answer to the question, Can I get what I want where I am? At the same time, begin an outreach process to determine if I might be better off leaving for another position in a new organization.	1. Within two weeks, meet with my current boss and someone in human resources to discuss my future potential within the organization. Prepare well for both discussions. Use the results of my life and career plan as key subject matter for those discussions. Success in this effort is solely defined as coming away knowing if I can achieve my life and career goals by staying with this organization. 2. Develop a systematic approach to a job search. This will include updating my résumé, making a list of everyone within my network and their contact information, testing my discussion points by seeking advice from individuals (not seeking a job), and working my way up to the most important discussions last, using early discussions as a way for me to learn how my approach to the job search is being received. 3. Within sixty days, decide if I should stay in my current organization or leave it. Have either a plan at work or a job search implemented within three months from now.

Model topic	Insights	Strategy	Goals and time line
Strengths and development areas	I have three specific areas requiring further personal development: increasing my emotional intelligence; learning more about the financial aspects of this business; understanding more about project management.	To focus on the three areas requiring personal development so that each of those areas can be strengthened.	1. Determine if my organization will support me in my effort to strengthen these three areas by either paying for it or allowing time to do it. By the end of next month, know whether I can attend a class or seminar on this subject or be tested on emotional intelligence. 2. In two weeks, ask a senior executive in the finance department if he or she would be willing to mentor me through a process of increasing my financial acumen. If not, determine if there is an adult education or college course I might take to do so, perhaps company paid. 3. By the end of the month, ascertain if human resources and my boss will support me in either engaging in project management training or assigning me to a project with a leader who is willing to mentor me through a project management process. 4. After taking the preceding actions, determine within three months if I will need to find another employer to gain the development that I need. If I do, construct my job-search plan.

These are brief examples, but you can follow that same format for any of the sections of the model that we worked on before. Document the amount of detail that makes you comfortable with being able to move ahead. By now, you should have a fairly good idea of where you need to prioritize your attention. Remember, this is not the last plan you will be developing. It is your first one, and it is important. Choose to focus on the areas that bother you, that need resolution, and that will help you to move toward your next position and your vision. Look for current opportunities that should be pursued in this plan. When you do this exercise, attach to each goal a time for beginning and ending, as well as any aspects of the goal that can be measured. Be as specific as possible, name names, dates, and expected outcomes. After you document what you want to do, ask yourself, "Is what I plan to do reasonable and attainable?"

**When you do things in the present that you can see,
you are shaping the future that you are yet to see.**

—Idowu Koyenikan, *Wealth for All*

Lastly, when you are finished documenting your plan, you need to prioritize the strategies, laying them out over the two-year period. For example, those that are precursors to other goals should be done first. Those that are of deepest concern to you should be done first. As you plan this out, for each quarter of the year, you should see some even distribution of the actions to be taken, so that at the end of the two-year period of your plan, each of the strategies you've chosen and the goals attached to them will have been completed. It could look something like the example on the following page.

My Strategies, Goals, and Actions

Year 1

Q1	Q2	Q3	Q4
Strategy: Goal: Actions:	Strategy: Goal: Actions:	Strategy: Goal: Actions:	Strategy: Goal: Actions:

Year 2

Q1	Q2	Q3	Q4
Strategy: Goal: Actions:	Strategy: Goal: Actions:	Strategy: Goal: Actions:	Strategy: Goal: Actions:

> The most difficult thing is the decision to act; the rest is merely
> tenacity. The fears are paper tigers. You can do anything you
> decide to do. You can act to change and control your life;
> and the procedure, the process is its own reward.
>
> —Amelia Earhart

As you proceed to implement the strategies and goals, additional insights will develop. For example, if you were working on your personal development areas and you found little or no support coming from inside your organization, what would that tell you? It might cause you to focus your efforts much more on a job search looking for a position that could enhance your experience. Or, in trying to build friendships, you find that there are not enough people interested in your idea of a poker club. However, several of the people you contacted play bridge, and they invite you to join them. Why not? It might not be your original goal, but it still fulfills the strategy of finding more friends. A new goal toward that end becomes learning to play bridge.

The important thing is to look back over your documentation for each of the model topics, pulling out the lessons and teasing out the strategies that are most important to you over the next two years and committing to specific goals that are time based.

Noah had a real problem selecting only six to eight strategies. He really wanted to get things done quickly. However, he was afraid that if he selected too many strategies, he would not be able to focus on any of them, and it would deflate his enthusiasm for action. Noah decided that he would prioritize just six areas and would do it in a way that would keep his level of interest up. He chose to act first on two areas of the plan where he felt it would be easier for him to take action and for him to achieve early success: "personal development" and "exploring new interests." The next four areas of the model he chose to include in his plan would be a bit harder for him, but these were areas that really bothered him and where he wanted to see progress. Those areas were "life balance," "improving or shedding a toxic relationship," "focusing on what he wanted for his next job," and "getting a long-delayed financial plan accomplished." Noah listed his strategies, goals, and actions by quarter for each of two years. The last four areas of focus would begin toward the end of the second quarter of the first year. He decided to take care of the "toxic relationship" and to "hire a financial planner" so that both would be resolved in the second half of the first year. He left "life balance" and "planning for his next job" to be the focus for the early part of the second year of his plan. This excited him. He had things to do, knew what he wanted to do, and understood that by accomplishing his goals, he would be moving toward his vision.

When at work, most people understand that planning is an important managerial process. It helps people in a business or company to focus on certain issues, while the planning itself is a learning process. Planning causes the organization to focus its questions and to create important assumptions. Isn't it just as important for individuals to do these very same things when planning for their life and career? We are also suggesting that, just as a business or organization might, you look at what is most urgent and important in your life and address those as early as possible. Think about seizing your opportunities while avoiding being distracted by less important issues. However, you might be a person like Noah and prefer to act first on one or two things that are likely to bring you early success. The decision is up to you.

A good plan uses assumptions that have been thought through. At this point, some of your assumptions might include the following: my vision is realistic; I can obtain the support that I need; my job and compensation desires are realistic; I can trust myself to act and accomplish my goals; I want to control as much of my future as possible. Test your own assumptions and make sure that you are honest with yourself. Also, remember that your assumptions can change and be updated as you move through the deployment of your plan. New learning informs new assumptions and plans.

Now it is time to begin your plan. Below is a chart providing space for you to choose six key strategy areas from your model topics. You may choose to use fewer or perhaps more, depending on your situation. However, try to select from the thirteen model topics a discrete number on which you want to work. Keep it to about six to eight at the most. You should stretch yourself but not overwhelm yourself.

We suggest you use the format below to document your plan; however, if you are familiar with or more comfortable with a different format for plan documentation, please use it. The most important thing is to document the details of your plan, since it will be used as your reference source over the next two years. In addition, the document needs to have space for recording monitored results. You can do this on paper, in a notebook, on your computer, or in any other way that makes you comfortable. Having easy access to the documentation while being able to record the result of your actions is the key. At a minimum, your plan should be updated every two weeks.

My Life and Career Plan

Document in each of the blank spaces below the model topic that you have chosen to include in your first action plan.	Document in each of the blank spaces below what insights or learning you uncovered in this model section.	Document in each of the blank spaces below the strategies that are important to you.	Document in each of the blank spaces below what goals and actions you will accomplish and when.	As you proceed with your plan and begin to achieve your goals or hit roadblocks, use this column to record your status.
Model topic	**Insights**	**Strategy**	**Goals and time line**	**Monitoring for results**

Model topic	Insights	Strategy	Goals and time line	Monitoring for results
Model topic	Insights	Strategy	Goals and time line	Monitoring for results
Model topic	Insights	Strategy	Goals and time line	Monitoring for results
Model topic	Insights	Strategy	Goals and time line	Monitoring for results

Sharing for Advice

Once you've completed your action plan, it's now time to share it with at least one key relationship in your life. Try reserving enough time with this person to review your entire life and career plan. Depending on the relationship and your approach to these kinds of discussions, you may or may not want to share a written document summarizing your plan in advance with your key relationship. Whether you share the information in advance or at the meeting, be open. Divulge to the person your concerns, insights, expectations, and plans. Let the individual know that your one and only interest, as a result of your respect for that person, is to seek his or her candid advice about each of the model topics, how you saw them, and the resultant strategies and goals you have developed.

As you open your plan for the person's review, be prepared with some key questions to help the conversation along. Here are a few:

- Do you see anything in this particular topic area that I am missing?
- Do you think that I am jumping to any conclusions, or am I making considered evaluations?
- Do my strategies and goals appear to be realistic to you?
- Have I missed any strategies or goals that you think should be in my plan?
- What advice do you have for me as a next step in my life and career development?
- Is there anyone else whom you would recommend that I talk to about this?
- Knowing me as you do, do you think I am on the right life and career track?

Take notes and document the feedback you are receiving during your meeting. This is not the time to qualify the advice you are getting or to agree or disagree with it. It is the time to clarify the advice, making sure that you understand what the individual is saying to you. It's also time to follow up with additional questions on the advice you've been given. Be sure to thank the person at the end of your discussion.

Let the person know that you will keep him or her informed of your progress.

Karl met with a trusted executive friend who works for Karl's previous employer. His friend Norma reviewed Karl's plan and discussed it with him. On the basis of her knowledge of his life and abilities, she recommended two things. Karl wanted to further develop his management skills; however, Norma thought that he should first spend time improving his knowledge of technology. In addition, Norma suggested that Karl stay with his current employer for one more year, and if by that time his career did not progress, he should consider moving on to another position outside the company. Norma knew the company that Karl now worked for, and she also knew Karl's skill and ability level. She felt that if he did not progress within a year, he would be better off moving elsewhere in their industry.

Karl listened intently and greatly appreciated Norma's input to the discussion. However, he decided that he still wanted to focus on improvement of his management skill and ability. Karl did feel that remaining one more year in his current position was good advice, and he decided to do that.

At this point, you have developed your plan, you have shared it, and you have received advice. You should have met with at least one of your key relationships. You have documented that input. At times, serendipity develops when you have conversations with several key relationships. For example, to your surprise, you might find out about job openings, whether within your company or outside it, that are enticing to you. These conversations could also lead to introductions to other people who might be helpful to you now and in the future. So the more of these discussions you can have, the better. Remember, you're asking for help and advice, and most people like to provide advice.

Now is the time to review your notes on these meetings, examine the feedback, and ask yourself whether your plan should be adjusted in any way. What changes can or should be made?

After you have adjusted your plan, it's time to put it into practice. All of your work to date represents the wind that's about to power your sails, moving you in the direction of your vision. You have adjusted your plan, you know the dates you are going to get started on your strategies and goals, and you know the people you are going to see and the things you are going to do, so take the first steps.

Recording the Implementation of Your Plan

Document the results of your actions at least every two weeks; document additional lessons learned; document changes to your plan as a result of what you learn as you move through the implementation of your plan. During the course of the two years of your plan implementation, stuff will happen. Use the plan as a decision-making tool as these things occur. For instance, say you get a new job offer. If you say yes, does it resolve any of the issues in your plan? Does it continue to place you on your road toward your vision? Or you're going to get married, but that necessitates a change of jobs and a move to a new state. Will the priorities and strategies in your plan now change? Or perhaps a values clash arises at work. This clash is so intense that you have to make decisions about how you will handle it even though it might have negative consequences on your career. How will your values help you?

So here's the sequence that we just went through in this book and that you should repeat for yourself every two years:

- You work through the Life & Career Planning Model, and if you're honest with yourself, you will learn what is important to you.
- You analyze your situation and your feelings, and you determine what areas require action based on your vision.
- You develop strategies and goals in those areas, you share them with at least one key relationship, you revise the plan if necessary, and you implement.
- As time passes, you achieve some of your goals, the environment changes around you, and you must adapt. This changes your plans.

We recommend to our clients that they review their life and career plan at least every two years and whenever a major life event occurs, determine what has changed, create a new action plan, and go though this whole process once again. It is much easier the second time around since you are reviewing the documentation from the first time, identifying anything that has changed, and then documenting the new information and any new actions needed going forward. We find that some goals might be carried over to the third or fourth year, and new goals are developed as a result of new information. The important thing is to treat the life and career action plan as a living document, used to make decisions, used to provide actionable guidance, and used to keep you on the path to your vision. So don't be dissuaded. Stay the course. Make the adjustments. Keep moving forward. If a major life event occurs, redo your plan and, if necessary, your vision. The Life & Career Planning Model will continue to inform you, motivate you, and guide you toward your best possible life.

An Excerpt from *Jonathan Livingston Seagull: A Story* by Richard Bach

The next night from the Flock came Kirk Maynard Gull, wobbling across the sand, dragging his left wing, to collapse at Jonathan's feet. "Help me," he said very quietly, speaking in the way that the dying speak. "I want to fly more than anything else in the world . . ." "Come along then," said Jonathan. "Climb with me away from the ground, and we'll begin."

"You don't understand. My wing. I can't move my wing."

"Maynard Gull, you have the freedom to be yourself, your true self, here and now, and nothing can stand in your way. It is the Law of the Great Gull, the Law that is."

"Are you saying I can fly?"

"I say you are free."

As simply and as quickly as that, Kirk Maynard Gull spread his wings, effortlessly, and lifted into the dark night air . . . "I can fly" . . . "I CAN FLY!"[1]

You can fly.

Remember that we want to help. If you get stuck, need advice, or want to seek more clarity, go to the resource listing at the back of the book. Take advantage of the cited reading material and websites, or contact us through our website for tools, advice, or telephonic coaching. Just don't stop. Get this done. It's your life. It's your career. Get the best life, the best career, and the best you!

Have a bias toward action—let's see something happen now. You can break that big plan into small steps and take the first step right away.

—Indira Gandhi

Conclusion

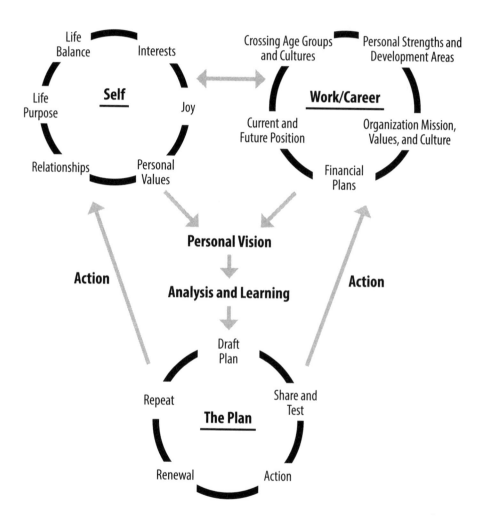

The image above shows the Life & Career Planning Model in its entirety. Until now, you've been working on one part at a time, isolated from the rest of the model, but when you see how the various sections work together, you can see how your self and work/career sections influence each other and your personal vision, and you can see how analysis of what you've learned leads to the development of the plan. When you take action on what you've planned, you influence the self and work/career parts of your life. They are all connected. You really cannot separate your work and career from your life outside of work. The ultimate purpose for using the Life & Career Planning Model is to better understand your personal life and career and how they are integrated. The model helps you to develop actions in a systematic way to achieve your life and career goals and, ultimately, to help you find your happiness.

Before I can tell my life what I want to do with it, I must listen to my life telling me who I am.

—Parker J. Palmer, *Let Your Life Speak*

To that end, you've reflected and spent time on those things in your life in which you have an *interest*, those aspects of your life that have given you *joy*. You've learned what drives you, your *personal values* and your *life's purpose*. You have also come to understand the importance of *life balance* and your many *relationships*. At the same time, you've given yourself a candid evaluation of your *personal strength and development areas* and how the *mission and culture* of the organization in which you work either supports or doesn't support you in your life goals.

A very important part of this book was meant to help you to determine if you have a *financial plan* and if that plan is strong enough to support you on the way to the personal *vision* you developed. You've taken a good look at your *current work position* and predicted what you would like your *future position* to be. As a result of *analyzing* your responses to the model topics, you've learned a great deal about yourself, where you are, and where you want to go. You've assimilated these *lessons* into an *action plan* containing specific *strategies and goals*. That plan has been helped along by conversations with *key relationships* and additional understanding of the *age groups and cultures* in which you are operating. So now you're about to *implement* your plan. However, as noted earlier, you're never really done with your life and career plan. You will need to *renew* it at least every two years or when a major life event occurs, updating it and drafting new plans, strategies, and goals to move you forward. Treat your plan as a live document and refer to it frequently as you take your actions.

Lisa, a thirty-eight-year-old executive, had completed her life and career plan eighteen months earlier. Suddenly she was faced with an unexpected pregnancy. At about the same time, her husband, Sam, received a job offer that required a move to another city. Lisa had shared her life and career plan with Sam, and he bought into it. Now the two of them were faced with decisions that might alter Lisa's plan, especially since her plan called for her to stay with her company in order to achieve the next executive level. When the plan was developed, children were not in the picture.

Lisa spent a good deal of time, both alone and with Sam, reviewing her life and career plan and discussing the potential that Sam had as a result of his new job offer. Several conclusions were reached. First, they were both very happy that a child was on the way. Second, Lisa did not want to give up her career and was willing to seek a transfer to another of her company's locations near where Sam would be employed. Sam agreed that he would accept the new position and commute back and forth on weekends until their child was born. At that time, they would sell their home, and Lisa would transfer or seek a similar position at the new location. Lisa's vision remained intact, while Sam satisfied his own career desires. Both were now also focused on building a family, not just a career. Lisa revised her life and career plan and took it out another two years.

Jonathan was in the second year of his third two-year life and career plan, when his wife, Samantha, passed away. At sixty years of age, he was facing a very different lifestyle than his plan had depicted. In reviewing his financial plan, his current health status, and his family relationships, he decided to redo his plan and to envision retirement within two years. Although it was much too early to think about another close relationship, he revised his plan to include consideration of such a relationship sometime in the second year of the new plan. He discussed his plan with two key relationships, his son, Lynn, and his daughter, Jane. These key relationships were important to him, as were his four grandchildren. His son and daughter gave him some direct and very important feedback on the plan, including telling him that he was still young and that although they had lost their mother, they hoped he might find another significant relationship in his future. Jonathan revised his plan, his personal vision, including interests during retirement, and set on a path to be as happy as he could be after a sad event because he knew his wife, Samantha, would have wanted it that way.

Lisa's and Jonathan's examples are merely two of the myriad types of changes that could occur in anyone's life. If you are lucky, your life road will be long, and many changes or side roads will appear along the way. How you navigate that journey is a really important aspect of taking as much control as possible over your future. Your life and career plan is a tool providing flexibility to help you ride the waves of change. Use it.

There is no passion to be found playing small—in settling for a life that is less than the one you are capable of living.

—Nelson Mandela

Both of us, Alex and Melissa, have been blessed to be able to help individuals along the way to their best life. You now have an opportunity to do the same thing. Share this book and what you have learned with others. Become the mentor you have always wanted to have. Be someone's key relationship; lead with your values, passion, and personal mission.

Congratulations for having stayed with this process even when it got tough to keep going. It shows that you care about yourself and you care enough to invest in both the present and future you. You now possess a tool for lifetime use. You're no longer in the group of individuals who see their life happening to them. You're now a member of the group of people who create a new life for themselves through their plans and actions. You can be the person that you want to be, and you've taken a most important step toward who you will become. You have also helped us to achieve our purpose of helping you to have the best life, the best career, and the best you.

Life isn't about finding yourself. Life is about creating yourself.

—George Bernard Shaw

Acknowledgments

Alex Plinio would like to thank Melissa Smith, without whose advice, counsel, and support this book would not have been published; my many enablers, including those at Allstate, Prudential Financial, American Field Service, the Institute for Ethical Leadership at Rutgers Business School; my clients and students for all of the experience and joint learning; and finally, my third-grade teacher, Mrs. Gogel, who saw in me things that others could not see and challenged me greatly to become all that I could be.

Melissa Smith would like to thank Alex Plinio, who first introduced me to Life & Career Planning, which has had such an important impact on my life, and for his friendship over the years and now partnership.

Notes

Introduction

1 Bureau of Labor Statistics, US Department of Labor, "The Employment Situation," Economic News Release, June 2018.

2 Bureau of Labor Statistics, US Department of Labor, "Number of Jobs, Labor Market Experience, and Earnings Growth among American at 50: Results from a Longitudinal Survey," Economic News Release, August 24, 2017.

3 2016 ICF Global Coaching Study, based on a 2015 survey commissioned by ICF and conducted by PricewaterhouseCoopers LLP.

4 David F. Larcker, Stephen Miles, Brian Tayan, and Michelle E. Gutman, *2013 Executive Coaching Survey* (Stanford, CA: Miles Group and Stanford University, August 2013).

Chapter 1   Interests

1 Alice G. Walton, "Phone Addition Is Real—And So Are Its Mental Health Risks," *Forbes*, December 11, 2017, https://www.forbes.com/sites/alicegwalton/2017/12/11/phone-addiction-is-real-and-so-are-its-mental-health-risks/#41ae8de113df.

Chapter 2   Joy

1 Sonja Lyubomirsky's home page: http://sonjalyubomirsky.com/ (accessed May 25, 2018).

2 Molly Simms, "What Would Make You Happy? We Signed Up for a 30-Day Course to Find Out," *O—Oprah Magazine*, May 2018, http://www.oprah.com/inspiration/laurie-santos-happiness-research.

Chapter 5   Life Purpose

1 Drew Hendricks, "Personal Mission Statement of 13 CEOs and Lessons You Need to Learn," *Forbes*, November 10, 2014, https://www.forbes .com/sites/drewhendricks/2014/11/10/personal-mission-statement-of -14-ceos-and-lessons-you-need-to-learn/#62986fd01e5e.

Chapter 6   Life Balance

1 Brian O'Connell, *Fifty Years in Public Causes* (Medford, MA: Tufts University Press, 2005), 71.
2 Rebecca Webber, "Mirror, Mirror," *Psychology Today*, December 2017, 56.

Chapter 8   Organization Mission, Values, and Culture

1 *BusinessDictionary*, s.v. "mission statement," accessed June 28, 2018, http://www.businessdictionary.com.
2 Bill George, *True North: Discover Your Authentic Leadership* (San Francisco: Jossey-Bass, 2015), 180.
3 Stephen R. Covey, *The 7 Habits of Highly Effective People* (New York: Simon and Schuster, 2018), 143.
4 CTE Resource Center, "An Organization's Values," accessed June 28, 2018, http://www.cteresource.org/attachments/atb/aai/organiz_values.pdf.
5 Jim Collins and Jerry Porras, *Built to Last: Successful Habits of Visionary Companies* (New York: Harper Business, 1994), 73–74.
6 Wells Fargo, "The Vision, Values & Goals of Wells Fargo," accessed January 17, 2019, https://www.wellsfargo.com/about/corporate/vision-and -values/.
7 Kevin McCoy, "Wells Fargo Fined $185M for Fake Accounts; 5,300 Were Fired," *USA Today*, September 29, 2016, https://www.usatoday.com/ story/money/2016/09/08/wells-fargo-fined-185m-over-unauthorized -accounts/90003212/.
8 Craig Giammona and Jacqueline Simmons, "Indra Nooyi, Pepsi's First Female CEO, Is Stepping Down," *Time*, August 6, 2018, http://time.com/ 5358550/indra-nooyi-pepsi-female-ceo/.

9 PepsiCo, "Our Guiding Principles," accessed January 17, 2019, https://www.pepsico.com/about/mission-and-vision.

10 Julie Creswell, "Indra Nooyi, PepsiCo C.E.O. Who Pushed for Healthier Products, to Step Down," *New York Times*, August 6, 2018, https://www.nytimes.com/2018/08/06/business/indra-nooyi-pepsi.html.

11 Daniel Goleman, Richard Boyatzis, and Annie McKee, *Primal Leadership: Unleashing the Power of Emotional Intelligence* (Boston: Harvard Business Review Press, 2013), 194.

Chapter 11   Crossing Age Groups and Cultures

1 Center for Women and Business, Bentley University, *Multi-Generational Impacts on the Workforce* (Waltham, MA: Center for Women and Business, Bentley University, Fall 2017), 1–2.

2 Judith L. Fenze, "Examining Generational Differences in the Workplace: Work Centrality, Narcissism, and Their Relation to Employee Work Engagement" (PhD diss., University of Wisconsin–Milwaukee, 2013), 21–24.

3 Center for Women and Business, *Multi-Generational Impacts on the Workforce*, 1–2.

4 Desda Moss, "5 Generations + 7 Values = Endless Opportunities," Society for Human Resources Management, June 20, 2017, http://SHRM.org.

5 David Livermore, *The Cultural Intelligence Difference* (New York: American Management Association, 2011), xiii.

6 John W. Traphagan, "A Simple Way to Increase Your Cultural Awareness at Work," Fast Company, March 20, 2015, https://www.fastcompany.com/3043687/a-simple-way-to-raise-your-cultural-awareness-at-work.

7 Cultural Intelligence Center, "What Is CQ?," accessed July 25, 2018, https://culturalq.com/what-is-cq/.

8 Richard D. Lewis, "The Lewis Model: Dimensions of Behavior," June 22, 2015, https://www.crossculture.com/the-lewis-model-dimensions-of-behaviour/.

9 Livermore, *Cultural Intelligence Difference*, 11–18.

Chapter 12   Personal Vision

1 Jim Collins and Jerry Porras, *Built to Last* (New York: Harper Business), 232, 233.

Chapter 14   Planning, Action, and Renewal

1 Richard Bach, *Jonathan Livingston Seagull: A Story* (New York: Avon, 1973), 194, 195.

Resources

Life & Career Planning, LLC

Alex and Melissa's firm, Life & Career Planning, provides consulting and coaching services to individuals, businesses, nonprofit organizations, and government agencies. The executive coaching service includes the use of the Life & Career Planning Model and is found to be exceptionally helpful and impactful for individuals seeking to enhance their current careers. Consulting services help executives and board leaders with their strategic issues such as organization development, succession planning, and change management. We also support organizations with our coaching process, which helps to drive individual managers and executives to higher levels of performance. For individuals, businesses, or organizations, see our contact information below.

We offer a broad array of services that can be deployed individually or in combination, including:

- Individual coaching. Work one-on-one in person with a life and career planning coach.
- Telephonic coaching. Wherever you live or work, receive one-on-one coaching via the telephone including Facetime or Skype.

Webinars

Spend an hour focused on a specific life and career planning topic such as personal values, the right job, life balance, strengths and development areas, organization culture and values, financial plans, your vision, crossing age groups and cultures, and your life and career plan action and renewal process.

Crisis and Opportunity Help Line

Clients or people seeking to become a client can email us and be guaranteed a call back within twelve hours to discuss challenges they face: contactus@lifeandcareerplanning.com.

Life and Career Planning Seminars

Invest a half day in your personal and professional success.

Life and Career Planning Retreats

Invest two days in your personal and professional success.

Presentations

We will come to your organization, association, or business and present to employees, management, or executives on any subject noted in the list of services above or below that we provide.

Governance

Working with a board of directors, our firm focuses with governance leaders on their challenges and future needs including board succession and development and individual executive or board member coaching.

Human Resources Issues

Our firm addresses human resources issues including team building, organization development, and business model alignment.

Management and Executive Coaching

We coach managers and executives in two ways: first, the individual develops a holistic life and career plan through self and career introspection; second, the managers or executives have an opportunity to work one-on-one with a coach to explore their current challenges and opportunities, discern potential options for themselves and their organizations, and make prudent decisions for implementation.

Employee Communications

Our firm has experienced communications professionals who help managers and executives develop ongoing employee communications programs and various approaches to obtain employee feedback on issues of importance to the organization.

Coalition Building

Individual organizations and groups of like-minded organizations and associations often find a need to coalesce around specific challenges—to implement change, to influence public policy, or simply to plan together for their uniform self-interest. Our firm has substantial experience in helping groups of various kinds find common ground and work together.

Meeting Facilitation

Most organizations understand that it can be highly productive to have an objective consultant facilitating important meetings and to help leaders prepare for those meetings. Our firm offers this service.

Life and Career Planning Course

For more information, see our website: Lifeandcareerplanning.com.

To contact us with questions, comments, or for appointments, email us: contactus@lifeandcareerplanning.com.

Books and Websites

Interests

If You Don't Know Where You're Going You'll Probably End up Somewhere Else by David Campbell, Sorin Book, 2007.
Living Your Best Life by Laura Berman Fortgang, Tarcher/Putnam, 2002.

Surveys

The Campbell Interest and Skill Survey (CISS), created by David P. Campbell, is a self-report instrument that measures work-related interest and skills to help guide an individual to a specific occupational area. The scales of the CISS are based on the individual's attraction to a career and his or her confidence in completing those activities. Counselors, psychologists, and human resource professionals use this instrument for displaced and transitioning employees, career development, personal counseling, and targeting academic study. https://goo.gl/a6ciEX.

The Strong Interest Inventory (SII) is an interest inventory used in career assessment. As such, once an individual's interests are assessed, that assessment may be used in career counseling. The SII is also frequently used for educational guidance as one of the most popular career assessment tools. https://goo.gl/EGHYg6.

Joy

The Book of Joy: Lasting Happiness in a Changing World by Dalai Lama, Desmond Tutu, and Douglas Carlton Abrams, Avery, 2016.
How Much Joy Can You Stand? A Creative Guide to Facing Your Fears and Making Your Dreams Come True by Susanne Falter-Barns, Ballantine/Wellsprings, 2000.

Personal Values

Giving Voice to Values: How to Speak Your Mind When You Know What's Right, by Mary Gentile, Yale University Press, 2010.
Meeting the Ethical Challenges of Leadership by Craig E. Johnson, Sage, 2017.

Values: The Secret to Top Level Performance in Business and Life by Dr. Betty Uribe, Next Century, 2017.

Mission or Purpose

Discover Your Purpose: How to Use the 5 Life Purpose Profiles to Unlock Your Hidden Potential and Live the Life You Were Meant to Live by Rhys Thomas, Tarcher/Penguin, 2015.

How to Develop Your Personal Mission Statement by Stephen R. Covey, Grand Harbor, 2013.

Relationships

I Hear You: The Surprisingly Simple Skill behind Extraordinary Relationships by Michael S. Sorensen, Autumn Creek, 2017.

"7 Key Habits for Building Better Relationships" by Harvey Deutschendorf, Fast Company, February 2, 2015, https://goo.gl/NBw5MG.

Social Intelligence: The New Science of Human Relationships by Daniel Goleman, Bantam, 2017.

Life Balance

The American Institute of Stress: https://www.stress.org/.

Off Balance: Getting Beyond the Work-Life Balance Myth to Personal and Professional Satisfaction by Matthew Kelly, Avery, 2011.

The Seven Spiritual Laws of Success: A Practical Guide to the Fulfillment of Your Dreams by Deepak Chopra, Amber-Allen, 1995.

Strength and Development Areas

Personal Development Simplified: An Easy to Follow Guide to Personal Development for Beginners; Identify and Break Negative Patterns; Become a Better Version of Yourself. Guaranteed by Kshitij Prasai, CreateSpace, 2017.

Working with Emotional Intelligence by Daniel Goleman, Bantam, 1998.

Self-Assessments

Self-Assessment/Strengths–Weaknesses by BilSE-Institut: https://goo.gl/
   bUiJFP.

Skills You Need: https://www.skillsyouneed.com/.

Strengths and Weaknesses Analysis by 123 test: https://goo.gl/5YLHUd.

Organizational Culture

*The Best Place to Work: The Art and Science of Creating an Extraordinary
   Workplace* by Ron Friedman, Perigee, 2015.

Built to Last: Successful Habits of Visionary Companies by Jim Collins and
   Jerry Porras, Harper Business, 1994.

Culture Wins: The Roadmap to an Irresistible Workplace by William Vander-
   bloemen, Savio Republic, 2018.

Financial Planning

The Balance: https://www.thebalance.com/.

"Build a Personal Finance Spreadsheet Model" by SpreadsheetSolving:
   https://spreadsheetsolving.com/personal-finance-modeling/.

CFP Board: https://www.cfp.net/home, http://www.letsmakeaplan.org/.

"Essential Components to a Financial Plan" by Hyre Personal Wealth Advisors: https://goo.gl/dawPhj.

"Insights" by Mercer Advisors: https://goo.gl/VZ7Nps.

Motley Fool, with investment, personal finance, and retirement advice:
   https://www.fool.com/.

The 9 Steps to Financial Freedom by Suze Orman, Crown Business, 2006.

"6 Elements of a Solid Personal Finance Plan" by The College Investor:
   https://goo.gl/NqXYpj.

Current and Future Position

Get a Life, Not a Job: Do What You Love and Let Your Talents Work for You
   by Paula Caligiuri, FT Press, 2010.

*The Pathfinder: How to Choose or Change Your Career for a Lifetime of Sat-
   isfaction and Success* by Nicholas Lore, Touchstone, 2012.

Online Job Sites
CareerBuilder: https://www.careerbuilder.com.
Dice: https://www.dice.com.
Glassdoor: https://www.glassdoor.com.
Google for Jobs: search "Google for Jobs."
Idealist: https://www.idealist.org.
Indeed: https://www.indeed.com.
Job.com: http://www.jobs.com.
LinkedIn: https://www.linkedin.com.
Monster: https://www.monster.com.
SimplyHired: https://www.simplyhired.com.
TheLadders: https://www.theladders.com.
Us.jobs: https://us.jobs.

Crossing Age Groups and Cultures

Beyond Race and Gender by R. Roosevelt Thomas Jr., American Management Association, 1991.

Generational Insights by Cam Marston, Generational Insights, 2010. Cam Marston is a leading expert on the impact of generational change and its impact on the workplace and marketplace: https://generationalinsights.com/.

Intercultural Competence by Myron W. Lustig and Jolene Koester, Pearson, 2012.

The Intercultural Group, specializing in cross-cultural training, cross-cultural coaching, and cross-cultural consulting: https://goo.gl/7oRQnc.

A Manager's Guide to Globalization: 6 Skills for Success in a Changing World by Stephen H. Rhinesmith, McGraw-Hill, 1996.

West Midland Family Center, with a complete chart of generational characteristics: https://goo.gl/BnA7GB.

Personal Vision

Principles and Power of Vision: Keys to Achieving Personal and Corporate Destiny by Myles Munroe, Whitaker House, 2015.

The Power of Habit: Why We Do What We Do in Life and Business by Charles Duhigg, Random House, 2012.

The 7 Habits of Highly Effective People by Steven R. Covey, Simon and Schuster, anniversary edition, 2013.

True North: Discover Your Authentic Leadership by Bill George, Jossey-Bass, 2007.

Planning, Action, and Renewal

MindTools: https://www.mindtools.com/pages/article/smart-goals.htm.

Smartsheet: https://www.smartsheet.com/blog/essential-guide-writing -smart-goals.

Search for a Coach

There are many different types of coaches, including executive coaches, life vision and enhancement coaches, leadership coaches, relationship coaches, and career coaches. You may want to partner with a coach to advance your own personal or professional growth in specific ways. Many organizations use professional coaches to help them advance business goals and objectives.

International Coach Federation: Washington, DC, 888-423-3131, 888-236-9292 (coach referral service), https://coachfederation.org/find-a-coach.

Alex Plinio and Melissa Smith: https://www.lifeandcareerplanning.com/about-us/.

About the Authors

Alex J. Plinio previously served as a faculty member of Rutgers Business School and currently is president of Life & Career Planning, LLC, a consulting firm that coaches and advises students, managers, and leaders on life and career planning and executives and their boards on organization and board development. Alex is the cofounder of the Institute for Ethical Leadership and the Center for Nonprofit and Philanthropic Leadership at Rutgers Business School. In these multiple capacities, Alex coaches and mentors leaders, emerging leaders, and students. Formerly, Alex was the president/CEO of AFS-USA, the largest nonprofit international and intercultural student-exchange program in the United States, doing business in fifty countries around the world. He previously held senior executive positions at Prudential Financial in the areas of insurance, investments, financial services and public affairs and was CEO for Prudential Annuity Services, a billion-dollar-revenue retirement products business. His business experience includes executive positions in marketing, operations and administration, change management, and start-ups. Alex served as vice president of marketing for the Prudential Assets Management Company. He launched and served as president of the Prudential Foundation, a philanthropic organization known for expanding education, supporting social services, and helping community-based initiatives to combat poverty.

Alex has served his community by founding and serving on the boards of many organizations devoted to community and economic development, youth, education, and the arts. He served as chairman of a public-private partnership, the Newark Collaboration Group, and as a founding board member and chairman of the Governor's Schools of New Jersey and nationally with Gifts in Kind Inc. and the Independent Sector. Alex also served on the board of the Council for Advancement and Support of Education (CASE), the Alvin Ailey Dance Theatre, the Corporate Advisory Groups of the Council on Foundations, the Conference Board, the United Negro College Fund, the national United Way, and the boards of the Alliance for International and Intercultural Education and the Association for International Practical Training.

As a faculty member, business leader, board member, consultant, and executive coach, Alex is frequently invited to speak at professional convenings and management retreats. He has authored and contributed to publications including *Resource Raising: The Role of Non Cash Contributions in Corporate Philanthropy* and the *International Journal of Disclosure and Governance* and was a regular columnist for *Fundraising Management Magazine*. Among his many honors, Alex is the recipient of the Private Sector Initiatives Award from the president of the United States and the Rutgers Outstanding Alumnus Award. He was honored by Thomas Edison State University with the Doctor of Humane Letters, Honoris Causa, for his distinguished record of state and national service. Alex served his country honorably as a member of the United States Air Force.

Melissa A. Smith is the managing director of Life & Career Planning, LLC. Melissa has spent her career leading and learning about leadership. She began her career in Cincinnati, Ohio, at the US Shoe Corporation, where she was involved in sales, marketing, training, and operations. In 1995, she became the national sales manager for the Easy Spirit retail stores and relocated to White Plains, New York. Four years later, she accepted the role of president of the Aerosoles retail stores and built a team that doubled sales and the number of store locations. During that time, Melissa counseled numerous employees at all levels on career development and growth to assist them in their professional journey.

In 2005, Melissa decided to pursue a new direction in her career and took a year and a half off to reorganize and reinvent. Since that time, she has served as the executive director of the Institute for Ethical Leadership at Rutgers Business School and is a graduate of the Leadership Newark fellows program, the former board chair for the Wellness

Community of Monmouth and Ocean Counties in New Jersey, a former board member and vice president of the Newark Arts Council, and a former board member of the Rutgers Business School Alumni Association and the Institute for Ethical Leadership at Rutgers. Melissa is now actively engaged in leadership and management consulting in the nonprofit sector. In this role, she has taught ethical leadership to thousands of Rutgers Business School undergraduate students. She leads multiyear leadership development programs for emerging leaders and nonprofit executives. These programs focus on personal and professional development and have resulted in significant progress for many participants. She regularly spends time on one-on-one coaching sessions with the participants. Melissa has also served on her town planning board and was the chair of the Women and Family Issues Committee for the New Jersey League of Women Voters.

Melissa holds a bachelor's degree in business management and marketing from the University of Tennessee–Knoxville and received an executive MBA from Rutgers Business School. She also served as the class president for the Rutgers Executive MBA program during her time as a student.

Melissa loves outdoor adventure, most recently trekking to Machu Picchu in Peru and climbing Mount Kilimanjaro in Africa.